MELTDOWN

MELTDOWN

ASPERGER'S DISORDER,
CHALLENGING BEHAVIOR,
AND A FAMILY'S JOURNEY
TOWARD HOPE

THE ORP LIBRARY

WRITTEN BY
JEFF KRUKAR, PH.D.
KATIE GUTIERREZ
WITH
JAMES G. BALESTRIERI

WRITERS OF THE ROUND TABLE PRESS
PO BOX 511
HIGHLAND PARK, IL 60035

Publisher	COREY MICHAEL BLAKE
Executive Editor	COREY MICHAEL BLAKE
Post Production	DAVID CHARLES COHEN
Directoress of Happiness	ERIN COHEN
Coordinator of Chaos	KRISTIN WESTBERG
Facts Keeper	MIKE WINICOUR
Front Cover Design	ANALEE PAZ
Interior Design and Layout	SUNNY DIMARTINO
Proofreading	RITA HESS
Last Looks	KRISTIN WESTBERG
Digital Book Conversion	SUNNY DIMARTINO
Digital Publishing	DAVID CHARLES COHEN

Printed in the United States of America
First Edition: January 2013
10 9 8 7 6 5 4 3 2

Library of Congress Cataloging-in-Publication Data
Krukar, Jeff
Meltdown: asperger's disorder, challenging behavior, and a family's
journey toward hope / Jeff Krukar and Katie Gutierrez
with James G. Balestrieri.—1st ed. p. cm.
Print ISBN: 978-1-939418-02-9   Digital ISBN: 978-1-939418-03-6
Library of Congress Control Number: 2012954217
Number 1 in the series: The ORP Library
The ORP Library: Meltdown

RTC Publishing is an imprint of Writers of the Round Table, Inc.
Writers of the Round Table Press and the RTC Publishing logo
are trademarks of Writers of the Round Table, Inc.

CONTENTS

INTRODUCTION

Today, according to the U.S. Department of Health and Human Services, more than 5.5 million children—or eight percent of kids—in the U.S. have some form of disability. Whether the problem is physical, behavioral, or emotional, these children struggle to communicate, learn, and relate to others. While there is no longer *segregation* in the same sense as there was in the 1950s, what remains the same is the struggle. Even with all of our resources and technology, parents of children with disabilities fight battles every day to find the help and education their children need.

I have led Oconomowoc Residential Programs (ORP) for almost thirty years. We're a family of companies offering specialized services and care for children, adolescents, and adults with disabilities. Too often, when parents of children with disabilities try to find funding for programs like ours, they are bombarded by red tape, conflicting information, or no information at all, so they struggle blindly for years to secure an appropriate education. Meanwhile, home life, and the child's wellbeing, suffers. In cases when parents and caretakers have exhausted their options—and their hope—ORP is here to help. We felt it was time to offer parents a new, unexpected tool to fight back: stories that educate, empower, and inspire.

The original idea was to create a library of comic books that could empower families with information to reclaim their rights. We wanted to give parents and caretakers the information they need to advocate for themselves, as well as provide educators and therapists with a therapeutic tool. And, of course, we wanted to reach the children—to offer them a visual representation of their journey that would show that they aren't alone, nor are they wrong or "bad" for their differences. What we found in the process of writing original stories for the comics is that these journeys are too long, too complex, to be contained within a standard comic. So what we are now creating is an ORP library of disabilities books—traditional books geared toward parents, caretakers, educators, and therapists, *and* comic books portraying the world through the eyes of children with disabilities. Both styles of books share what we have learned while advocating for families over the years while also honestly highlighting their emotional journeys. We're creating communication devices that anyone can read to understand complex disabilities in a new way.

In an ideal situation, these books will be used therapeutically, to communicate the message, and to help support the work ORP and companies like ours are doing. The industry has changed dramatically and is not likely to turn around any time soon—certainly not without more people being aware of families' struggles. We have an opportunity to put a face to the conversation, reach out to families, and start that dialogue.

Caring for children with disabilities consumes your life. We know that. And we want you to realize, through these stories, that you are not alone. We can help.

Sincerely,
Jim Balestrieri
CEO, Oconomowoc Residential Programs
www.orplibrary.com

A NOTE ABOUT THIS BOOK

Asperger's disorder is a complex syndrome that affects children in different ways. The child with Asperger's disorder depicted in the following story struggles with significant emotional and behavioral difficulties that require a therapeutic environment. The great majority of children with Asperger's disorder do not resemble the child shown in this story. But those who do resemble him face challenges that have made it difficult to benefit from education in the public school system. At Genesee Lake School, we strive to build relationships with the children in our care so that they learn new skills that will lead to a successful return to their home, school, and community. It is our hope that the following story will add to your own understanding of the often lonely journey experienced by families with children with these unique challenges and gifts.

PART I
THE DIAGNOSIS

"Benjamin."

He heard the sound, three beats, his name, but it didn't interest him. Neither did the voice, his father's. He was sitting cross-legged on the floor of his room, snapping pieces of a train track into place. They made a satisfying clicking noise each time—*clu-click, clu-click*—soothing like a metronome, and steadily the track was taking its predictable winding shape. The cars were lined up against the wall by color: red with red, blue with blue, silver with silver. Everything orderly and neat. When the track was ready, he would put the cars in the right sequence and—

"Benjamin!"

His father's voice was louder now. Benjamin looked up and paused with a wooden piece in his hand.

"Breakfast time! Hurry up or you'll be late."

It was time for breakfast. Breakfast was with Mom every day. Mom always came into his room and swooped his hair from one side to the other and said, "Benjamin, your breakfast is ready. It's your favorite—French toast." Every day she said it. Every day he followed her into the kitchen and sat at his chair, and she handed him the curved bottle of maple syrup and he squeezed three quick times on each piece, and then he set the bottle down and picked up his fork and ate. Every day was the same thing, and that was the way he liked it.

But today it was Dad in the kitchen, not Mom, and he didn't know why. Dad stood by the stove in his dark suit, broad shoulders to the doorway as he stirred something in a bowl. The smell of something-not-French-toast rose from the pan as Dad poured batter. Benjamin felt a prickle of unease. This might be pancakes, and he didn't like them.

"Where is Mom this morning?" he asked.

Dad turned from the stove, gesturing Benjamin to the table with a spatula. "I thought we told you," he said. "Mom had to go to the doctor. Sit down with your sister. I'll bring your breakfast over."

"No," Benjamin said, rooted in place. His eyes were fixed on the clock above Dad's shoulder. The little hand was on the seven. The big hand was on the six. "I always have French toast, and those are pancakes."

"Benjamin, I can't make everyone a different breakfast. I'll be late for work. These are blueberry pancakes. The blueberries are even from our garden. Now sit down at the table with Mandy and eat."

Benjamin's older sister Mandy looked up from her coloring book. The corners of her mouth turned down. "Dad, Benjamin always eats French toast for breakfast. I mean *always*. Like every day. He eats it on his train plate. He likes to pour the syrup—"

"I know what your mom makes him, but I'm not Mom." Dad slid a pancake onto a growing stack. He brought the plate to the table and set it in the middle, kissing the top of Mandy's head. "This is a good breakfast, too. He can't have the same thing every day. No one can, and it's not even healthy. He needs to learn to be flexible." To Benjamin, he added in a teacherly voice, "It's good to be thrown a curve ball once in a while in life. I know I've been thrown a few."

"But Dad—" Mandy tried, looking at Benjamin. He was starting to pace.

"Just eat your breakfast," he said. "Benjamin. Stop that. Come over here, sit down, and eat."

Benjamin looked at the table. There was a blue plate in front of his seat, not his train plate. Where was his train plate? And the blue plate was empty and shiny. There was no French toast, only that stack of pancakes. This was not like it usually was—it was wrong. Plus, Dad was talking about curve balls, and that made no sense at all; this was about breakfast. His chest felt tight, and he shook his head. Dad was doing this ALL WRONG. Benjamin paced more quickly, one end of the kitchen to the other.

"No." Benjamin's voice was loud. "I don't want pancakes. Mom always makes me French toast."

"Benjamin—" Dad's eyebrows were mushed close together. A vertical line formed between them as he walked over to Benjamin and put his hands on his shoulders, holding Benjamin in place. "I'm not going to tell you again. Sit down and—"

"NO!" Benjamin screamed, jerking away. "NO NO NO NO NO NO NO!"

He ran to the table and grabbed the blue plate, the wrong blue plate, and hurled it back at the cabinet. The plate was plastic, so it didn't break, but it made a loud sharp banging noise against the wood cabinet doors, and he slapped his palms against his ears to close out all the commotion—the plate hitting the cabinet, Dad's bad word, Mandy's high-pitched yell—and let himself drop onto the floor and roll into a ball and rock. He clenched his eyes shut, willing all of them to go away, willing his train plate to be in front of him, with his French toast on top of it, because that was the *right* way to have breakfast, the day couldn't start without it, and *why didn't they just keep things the way they were supposed to be?*

...

"Why in the world didn't you just make him his usual breakfast, Jason?" Benjamin's mom, Marie, asked her husband. They were standing in their bathroom, door closed and water running. It was where they went to talk about sensitive matters, since Benjamin had eerily sharp hearing. "He was off the whole day. The whole day was off balance and wasted because you wanted him to learn to be *flexible?* Benjamin doesn't do flexible, we know that."

"Well, maybe he's different because we allow him to get his way," Jason said. It was nine at night and he was just loosening his tie. "The more we give him what he wants, the more he'll repeat his behaviors." Almost as an afterthought, he added, "They were talking about this on one of those parenting shows on TV."

Marie sat on the ledge of the bathtub. She sighed as she met Jason's eyes in the mirror. "It's not that simple," she said. "He's not doing this on purpose. I don't believe he wants to get that upset, nor does he want to make us angry. He just has a hard time with change. I feel awful for forgetting to tell him about my appointment. This is all my fault."

4

Benjamin had been a very different infant, then toddler, than Mandy. He didn't play like other kids; at the Friday morning play group at the community center, he seemed to be in his own little world while Mandy was always making up a game with the other kids. When he did play with Mandy, there wasn't much "back and forth." He got stuck on certain toys, exploding if she changed the play in any way. Once, he punched her arm when she said train time was over and it was time to play cars and trucks.

"Every child is different," they used to say to each other. Of Benjamin's clumsiness, Jason added, "My parents told me it took a while for me to come around, too, and that I had a hard time skipping in gym class. Some kids are just late bloomers."

Despite their "late bloomer" theory, Benjamin had learned words pretty early. He knew quite a few phrases when he was two years old and was talking in complete sentences by three. After so much worrying about the way he interacted with other kids, Marie and Jason were relieved; Benjamin's grasp of language meant he was smart. Still, though some of the words he used were fairly advanced for a toddler, they weren't always put together in the right way. He also seemed to have problems understanding even shorter sentences they said to him. This simply added to Benjamin's other strange behaviors: his problem with eye contact—the way he gazed left or right instead of directly at a person; his sensitivity to tags and seams in clothing; not wanting to play with other kids; and exploding when he couldn't get his way, his tantrums so much more extreme than Mandy's had been. They'd so hoped Benjamin would grow out of these behaviors, but as he got older, the problems only grew with him.

Marie put a hand on her belly over her bathrobe. "Jason, what will we do if our next child is like Benjamin?" She looked away, trying not to cry. She was ashamed to admit to her husband that she hoped their third child would be nothing like their second. "I love him so much, but sometimes it's so hard ..."

Jason shook his head and put his arms around Marie. "It'll be all right."

. . .

Benjamin was six and Mandy eight when their little brother Zach was born. Benjamin's mom had read him books and shown him pictures about babies, explaining that Benjamin would be a big brother now. Benjamin didn't understand why Mom and Dad wanted to bring a baby into their house. He didn't know why people wanted babies at all. Babies didn't *do* anything, and you couldn't do anything with babies. They also made a lot of noise, and things changed a lot around the house. But Mom said Benjamin would be able to show his little brother how to play with trains and tell him how they worked, and Benjamin brightened.

"There is a train track close to our house," Benjamin said. "We can bring the baby to see the Burlington Northern Santa Fe line or the CSX. Burlington locomotives are orange and black, and the CSX ones are blue and yellow. Just like this picture." He offered her a picture of trains he'd cut from a book.

"That's right, honey." Mom took one of Benjamin's hands and put it on her big round belly. Benjamin liked the pressure of his hand between Mom's palm and stomach. "You'll be able to talk to your little brother about all of that."

But Mom was wrong. The first time Benjamin tried talking to his little brother about trains, his little brother opened his mouth and let out the ugliest, most piercing noise Benjamin had ever heard. Mom was holding Zach on the couch, and Benjamin immediately put one hand to his own ear and clapped another hand against the baby's mouth. Instantly his palm was slimy with drool. Benjamin hated the slipperiness and pressed harder so he wouldn't feel it.

"Quiet!" he said. "Be quiet! Stop yelling like that!"

"Benjamin!" Mom's voice was loud. She swiped Benjamin's hand away from the baby's mouth, and the baby kept making the horrible sound. "You don't cover your brother's mouth, not ever! Do you understand me?"

The noise, the noise, the noise: WAAAAAAAAAH-hiccup-WAAAAAAAAAAH. Benjamin swung his head from side to side.

"NO NO NO, this is too loud," he said. "I want quiet! Quiet! Quiet!"

The baby didn't stop crying, and Mom held it close to her. When Benjamin looked at Mom's face, he saw tears in her eyes and didn't understand why. When she opened her mouth, he pressed his hands harder to his ears, almost expecting her to make the same screaming sound as the baby.

"Go to your room, Benjamin, right now," she said instead. She sniffed. "I'm giving you a time out. I'll call you for dinner later."

Benjamin looked at them for a minute longer, baffled. Unlike the train track, this didn't make sense, and he couldn't put the pieces together. Still upset, but without saying a word, he turned and walked to his room.

...

Marie tried to dismiss the first incident of Benjamin's aggression toward Zach as normal middle child jealousy that got out of hand. Her girlfriends reassured her that their children had reacted the same way to the births of younger siblings. But Marie once again thought of Mandy, who had been loving and nurturing toward Benjamin since he was still in the womb.

"Let's read to him, Mommy," Mandy would say, and they would sit in the corner of Mandy's playroom, cuddled against pillows, and read to the baby in Marie's belly. When he was born, Mandy touched him gingerly, with reverence. She was only two at the time, but she seemed to have an innate knowledge that Benjamin was delicate, completely defenseless.

Benjamin had no such instinct. He was not interested in the baby at all before he was born, and all he seemed to feel toward his younger brother now was anger and resentment. Once, Marie stepped away from Zach for just a second, just to grab a diaper, and when she returned, Zach was wailing beneath the pillow Benjamin held over his face. Another time, when she was bathing Zach, Benjamin asked Marie in a tone of detached curiosity, "Mom, is it possible for babies to cry underwater?" Marie looked at Benjamin, who was gazing somewhere above her right shoulder, and a chill swept through her. Why did he act this way? What was wrong with her son? Where had she gone wrong?

"No, Benjamin," she said. "They can't. Babies can't cry underwater."

When she started continuously worrying about her infant's safety, Marie couldn't deny anymore that Benjamin's "difference" was something serious.

"Jason, we need to get some help for Benjamin," she said to him in their bathroom.

Jason didn't say anything for a bit. He just paced the small area, three strides taking him from one end to the other. "Help? What do you mean 'help'? What kind of help? We help him here."

"I don't know," Marie said. "I think he needs to see someone. We need to take him to a doctor."

"We took him when he was younger," Jason said. "When he didn't seem interested in others. His pediatrician said he was a little late in development."

"Yeah, but he's not acting like normal kids his age. Trying to hurt his baby brother isn't normal. Jason, what if we let it go too long? What if something is seriously wrong?" In a lower voice, Marie added, "What if it's something . . . *psychological?*"

They faced each other, and Jason put his hands on her shoulders. His face was drawn, and he looked very tired. "We'll figure this out. Let's take him back to his pediatrician and see what he says. Dr. Smith knows him best."

. . .

School started a week ago. At the playground during recess, just outside the entrance to the school, Benjamin stood to the side of a group of kids playing tag. They ran all around each other, with one chasing the others.

"Tag!" the boy yelled, catching up to another kid. "You're it!"

Benjamin wanted to play. The game seemed easy enough; all he had to do was run in and do what the last boy had done—"tag" someone. Then he was supposed to run away.

He dashed into the fray, slapping a palm against another boy's back. "Tag!" Benjamin shouted. "You're it!"

The boy stared at him. "You can't do that! You're not even playing with us!"

"Yes, I am," Benjamin said, confused. "I'm playing with you now. I tagged you. You're it!"

Just then, the boy who had first been tagged ran up and tagged the boy Benjamin had found. "You're it," he said smugly, before running away.

"Now look what you did!" the boy said to Benjamin. "You're such a loser! We don't even like to play with you!"

A handful of kids nearby laughed, and the boy darted off to join the rest of the group. Benjamin watched them. He ran through everything in his mind. He had done everything exactly the same as the other kids. What had gone wrong?

BRRRRRIIIIIIIIING!

It was the bell. The sound made Benjamin clap his hands over his ears. It was as if it were vibrating in his head, a gong crashing from one temple to the other. All around him, children streamed toward the entrance of the school, shrieking and yelling. Someone jostled Benjamin, knocking him off balance, and he pressed his hands harder to his ears. He didn't like this. It was chaos, a hurricane, trains crashing, and he was the only one who could feel it. Dimly, he heard a noise, mewling like a cat. It took him a moment to realize it came from him.

A playground aide noticed Benjamin standing alone and approached him. She put a hand between his shoulder blades and rubbed up and down. The firm, rhythmic motion calmed Benjamin long enough for him to glance at her. She smiled at him.

"Come on, sweetie. That bell is kind of loud, I know. It's time to go inside now."

. . .

Marie didn't realize that the first doctor's appointment would lead to another and then another. His pediatrician had said he had a possible sensory integration disorder and requested an occupational therapy evaluation, referring Marie to a clinic where she had taken Benjamin twice now. She was still on maternity leave but worried about what she would do once she started work again; she couldn't afford to take this much time off, and neither could Jason, who was in the middle of a big project at his engineering firm. She also didn't want to be constantly taking Benjamin out of school, but for now, it was the only way.

The first formal diagnosis came from an occupational therapist who said that Benjamin had a sensory integration disorder. That was why, she said, he got so upset about the feel of his clothes on his skin and also why he had such a hard time calming down when he was upset. He would need therapy sessions with her and to practice exercises at home.

The OT was a woman in her early thirties whom Benjamin took to immediately for some reason. He seemed to look at her more when she spoke, and he willingly carried out the therapy she recommended.

"Okay Benjamin. Look at this ball. Hold it and squeeze it hard," the OT said. She pressed a squishy blue ball into Benjamin's hand and held one in her own. "Like this." She curled her fingers around it and squeezed tightly.

Benjamin imitated her motion.

Beyond the squishy ball, she had him do all sorts of things: she asked him to climb jungle gyms and roll around in different materials, the latter of which Benjamin didn't like. He screamed as if he were being burned any time his skin touched a non-cotton fabric, melting into a puddle on the ground. His shrieks and cries made a headache immediately burst in Marie's temples, and if they were at home, little Zach burst into wails as well. Marie didn't know how long they would be able to keep him in therapy; Jason's family health insurance did not cover all of the cost, and the co-pay was expensive. For now, though, she spent the time in the waiting room, cuddling with Zach and enjoying the peace and quiet, even if it was just for an hour at a time. Some days, even after an occupational therapy session, she felt so overwhelmed that she locked herself in the bathroom for a few minutes. She realized she was doing that more and more these days.

The next diagnosis came when Benjamin was in second grade. If he was doing something he enjoyed—like science or history—he was extremely focused. Otherwise, he was often unable to keep up with the rest of the class, had a hard time following teacher directions, stared out the window, talked out of turn, and left his seat without permission. He also continued to throw tantrums when it was time to stop one activity—especially if it was of high interest—and start another. The school told Marie and Jason that this behavior might be more than what the OT was working on, that it was creating a problem for the other kids, and that they should have Benjamin evaluated. Feeling defeated, Marie and Jason returned to the pediatrician, where they talked for a while and filled out some rating scales. That was when Dr. Smith diagnosed

Benjamin with Attention Deficit-Hyperactivity Disorder—
and suggested that they consider giving him Ritalin.

"I'm not prepared to medicate our child," Marie said
staunchly to Dr. Smith. "He's only *seven*."

Jason agreed. "Absolutely not. Once you start on the
path of prescription medication, there's no going back.
Pills aren't a cure. It turns into a pill for everything instead
of working on the behavior itself."

Dr. Smith sighed. "I hear this from parents a lot, and I
understand your concerns. But I encourage you to have
the prescription filled and to consider using it if things
worsen at school and home."

If things worsen at school and home. Marie didn't like the
ominous sound of that.

Sure enough, Benjamin continued to have frequent,
now almost daily, meltdowns. The triggers varied, but
they included things they knew—such as loud noises, unexpected changes to his routine, and certain clothing—
as well as things they couldn't understand. Sometimes
Benjamin seemed to get mad out of the blue and way
out of proportion to what was going on at the time. One
afternoon, he had a huge meltdown directly after recess
when the teacher told the class to sit down, take out their
social studies notebook and a red pencil, and turn to the
last page. It almost seemed as if too much information
was being thrown at him, Marie thought later.

Marie returned to work, but the calls from Benjamin's
school pulled her from work at least once a week, and the
principal, while supportive for now, did not seem pleased.
It seemed as though she and Jason weren't talking about
anything but Benjamin and his problems, and they ar-
gued often about the right path to pursue. Marie had cried

more often over the past six months than she ever had, and Jason spent more time in his workshop than in the house when he wasn't at the office. Meanwhile, Mandy was virtually becoming a little second mother to Zach. He seemed to be well adjusted except for increased clinginess with Marie, though Mandy herself was less social than she used to be. Finally, Marie and Jason returned to a discussion about the Ritalin. Despite their misgivings, they decided to give it a try.

. . .

Benjamin really didn't like school. It was not fun. He tried and tried to make friends, but no one wanted to be friends with him, and he didn't understand why. He watched the other kids talk and laugh, but he didn't get what was funny. Sometimes he tried to laugh, too, imitating the exact number of ha-ha-has of another kid, but they always got quiet and looked at him strangely and walked away. Sometimes they called him a weirdo or a freak. Benjamin didn't like those words. Once, they told the teacher, "Benji's making fun of us!" and Benjamin yelled back, "My name is *Benjamin, not Benji!*"

"Inside voice, Benjamin," the teacher said.

Benjamin rocked slightly in his chair.

"Benjamin." She walked over to his desk from the front of the room. "Stop that. Look at me, Benjamin. Focus on me."

Benjamin didn't like looking at people's eyes. He didn't know why everyone always told him to do it. At home, Mom got close to him and held two fingers in front of his eyes, slowly drawing them nearer to her own. "Focus, Benjamin," she would say in a soft voice. But why did he need his eyes to focus his ears?

"Benjamin, I'm talking to you," the teacher said. He ignored her. Then she touched his shoulder.

"NO!" Benjamin screamed, recoiling. "No, you don't! Don't touch me!" He flailed his arms to move her away, and one of his hands smacked against her glasses. He kept screaming and flailing, knocking his chair over, and ran to the other side of the room. There was a window. He wanted to get away from here now.

"Benjamin!" the teacher yelled. "Look at what you did! You cut me! That's it! You're going to the principal's office and we're calling your mother to come get you. *Again!*"

Without looking, Benjamin could feel her getting closer and he didn't want her closer; he wanted to GET AWAY, so Benjamin hit the window as hard as he could with his fist. The glass didn't break, but a searing pain in his knuckles made him yowl. He hit the window again. He wanted to get away. He wanted to get away.

• • •

A few weeks later, Marie had arranged childcare for Mandy, now ten, and Zach, now two, and Jason took the afternoon off work so they could take Benjamin to a child psychologist a friend had recommended. Benjamin's school psychologist had mentioned that he shared qualities of kids with an autism spectrum disorder—such as poor social skills, adequate verbal skills, preoccupation with certain activities and subjects, and inflexibility—but the school's special education director had disagreed. Marie and Jason were frustrated to a point of desperation. They wanted a new, objective opinion.

They were silent in the car as they drove to pick up Benjamin from school. Their son looked tired and anxious as he climbed into the car.

"How was school today?" Jason asked.

Marie twisted to look at Benjamin in the backseat. He was chewing his lip, rocking slightly the way he'd been doing more lately.

"Honey, are you all right? Dad asked you how school was today," Marie prompted.

Benjamin looked out the window. Then he spoke as he always did, in a very precise manner with stress on almost all of the words. "When the bell rang in the morning, I went inside to the classroom. The bell was loud. The classroom is the third door inside the main entrance. The door has a small window in it. I hung my backpack on a hook and sat at my desk. There are four desks pushed together. We did our subjects. We did reading, math, social studies, and science. The boy next to me smells like dirt, Mom."

"That's not a nice thing to say, Benjamin," Marie said.

"It's true, though. This is not the way we go home."

"We talked about this, Benjamin," Jason said, glancing at him in the rearview mirror. "Remember?"

Benjamin rocked back and forth a bit. "You told me we're not going home after school today. We're going to see a new doctor. Then we're going home after I talk to the new doctor. I don't want a shot."

"That's right, and no shots. He's not that kind of doctor. It'll be fine," Jason said.

"If you turn left at the green light and then go straight and then turn right, we will be at Mandy's school."

Marie and Jason looked at each other, startled. Benjamin had only been to Mandy's school once, for a Christmas play two years ago.

"Right again, buddy," Jason said. His shoulders relaxed slightly; whatever else was going on with Benjamin, he was undeniably bright in certain ways: he had an impeccable memory for directions and other facts and had incredible hearing. Jason just hoped other things would improve for his son, like the anger issues and trouble making friends. Jason looked again at Marie, who was sitting rigidly, her hands folded in her lap. She seemed tense all the time lately. "We're almost to the doctor's office."

"We're not going to see Dr. Smith this time," Benjamin reiterated.

"No, not Dr. Smith. He's your pediatrician. This is a talking doctor. We're just going to have a conversation about how things are going with you."

"We're just going to have a conversation about how things are going."

In Dr. James's office, Marie pulled a thickening binder from her shoulder bag. She had started keeping a collection of Benjamin's paperwork, reports, evaluations, diagnoses, and recommendations. It was bad enough that she didn't know how to help her son or family, but she felt more inadequate when she didn't know the answer to a new doctor's question about her son's medical history. At least with her binder, she felt like somewhat of an expert on her son. That helped.

The receptionist watched over Benjamin in the waiting room while Marie and Jason first met with Dr. James. He was middle-aged, with kind eyes behind rimless glasses, and offered them a seat on a leather couch in his office.

"I know we talked briefly on the phone about Benjamin, but tell me more about how I can help you folks," he said.

"Well—this is the third time this month we've been

called to pick Benjamin up from school," Marie began. She thought of Benjamin, his little right hand wrapped in a white bandage, and felt a surge of frustration and sorrow. "This last time, they even called the school liaison police officer from the high school next door. When I got there, Benjamin was sitting in a corner by himself, crying. The school doesn't know what to do with him. We don't, either."

Dr. James nodded sympathetically. "From talking to you on the phone, it sounds like there has been some mention of school folks thinking your son might have characteristics associated with an autism spectrum disorder, right? Has there been any talk about a referral for special education?"

"No," Jason said, somewhat defensively. "Even with the ADHD, the teachers say his academics are grade and age appropriate. He's really smart. It's just these tantrums."

"And he's so impulsive when he's mad that he hurts himself in the process of trying to do other things, like run away," Marie added. "That's the worst part for me. Can you help us?"

"I hope so, and I believe I can," Dr. James said. "Let me meet briefly with your son, and then we'll go from there, okay?"

"Sure," said Jason. He and Marie went to the waiting room while Benjamin shuffled in his clumsy way into Dr. James's office. Dr. James closed the door behind him.

"What are they going to talk about in there anyway?" Jason asked, somewhat irritably.

"I don't know. I just hope we get some answers and some help."

"Benjamin needs the help, not us, Marie."

Marie gave a short laugh. "I'm not exactly feeling like

the epitome of maternal strength right now."

After meeting with Benjamin, Dr. James asked Marie and Jason to come back into the office while Benjamin returned to the waiting room. Marie smiled at him encouragingly, but he just glanced at her and then moved toward the pile of magazines on an end table.

Dr. James waited until Marie and Jason were settled again on the couch before he began. "From looking through the records you sent me, talking with you, and meeting your son, I'd like to recommend a comprehensive diagnostic assessment to evaluate your son's overall presentation and then make recommendations from there."

"Okay," Jason said. "Comprehensive diagnostic assessment. What does that entail?"

"Ideally, it requires multiple sessions—at home and school—over the course of several weeks, but it looks like your insurance will only cover a total of six hours for the entire evaluation. We'll have to space out the testing, other assessments, and report accordingly."

"Will six hours be enough?" Marie gestured to her binder. "We've been through so much already. I'd hate to go through the whole thing and then hear that more is needed but can't be done."

"And what about the—" Jason clenched his jaw. "The autism thing?"

"We'll take it one step at a time," Dr. James said, "but based on what we've discussed, as well as the behavior rating scales that you completed, I agree it would be a good course of action to assess characteristics of a possible autism spectrum disorder. Perhaps Asperger's disorder."

"Asperger's disorder," Jason repeated. Again, his tone was defensive.

Dr. James nodded. "Like I said, we'll take it one step at a time. Now, if it's okay with you, I'd like to observe you all playing together."

Jason shrugged. "I don't know what that's going to show, but if you think it will help ..."

Dr. James called Benjamin in from the waiting room and brought the family a basket of toys. "Here you go, Benjamin," he said, smiling supportively at Marie and Jason. "Why don't you see what toys you want to play with? There's a lot to choose from."

With that, he stood back a bit to observe.

In truth, Marie couldn't remember the last time they had "played" as a family. Benjamin didn't function that way. Still, she picked out a stuffed elephant, and Jason pulled out an action figure. Benjamin removed one toy after another from the basket, setting them down neatly beside each other, until he arrived at an airplane the size of his forearm. He held it with two hands, staring intently.

"Mr. Elephant would like to fly in your airplane, Benjamin," Marie said. Her voice was falsely bright.

"No, he doesn't," Benjamin said. "My airplane is too small." He twisted the airplane to remove its nose and set it down by his knee.

"My guy doesn't need a plane to fly," Jason said. He lifted the action figure and swooped it through the air in front of Benjamin, hoping to catch his son's attention.

Benjamin removed another part of the plane and set it by the first.

For the next ten minutes, Marie and Jason tried in vain to engage Benjamin in make-believe play. The three of them sat beside each other on the floor, but the truth was that if this were a photo, you could cut Marie and Jason out and Benjamin would not look out of place alone. His actions would not change. While he flew his plane parallel to their characters, there was no interaction between them.

"My plane is establishing air superiority," Benjamin said. "It takes a very skilled pilot. Oswald Boelke was one of the best fighter pilots in World War One."

Jason seized on the facts Benjamin presented. "You see how smart he is?" he asked.

Dr. James smiled and nodded. "Indeed."

Benjamin stood and led the plane in swirls through the air. Then he made a crashing sound as he brought the nose of the plane to the wall and let it drop.

"That's good, Benjamin." Dr. James sifted through the toys on the floor until he found a checkerboard. "Let's do this now. Do you know how to play checkers?"

Benjamin didn't look at him. He picked up his plane from the floor and continued flying it around the room.

After the session, Marie felt a combination of deflation and relief. Clearly, Benjamin didn't play the way other kids played—but at least he was acting here as he did at home, *and* there were no meltdowns.

"I'm afraid we're out of time for today," Dr. James said. "I'd like to see Benjamin alone next week for a play-based observation."

．．．

Benjamin was back in Dr. James's office. He sat on the same spot on the couch as he had last time, even though Mom and Dad weren't in the room. He didn't mind being here. Dr. James was nice (not like the kids at school), and Benjamin was eager to talk about his favorite subject.

"Railroads called wagonways were used in Germany as early as 1550," he said.

Dr. James looked at his watch.

"They were not like our railroads today. They were wooden, and it was not trains that used them—it was horse-drawn carts."

As Benjamin talked, Dr. James stood up and walked around the room. He turned his back on Benjamin and looked at his bookshelves.

"Iron replaced wood on the railroads in 1776."

"Okay, Benjamin," Dr. James said. "That's good. Let's do something else now. Let's play with blocks."

Benjamin didn't want to play with blocks. He didn't move from the couch, even when Dr. James spread a pile of blocks on the carpet before him.

"Do you like building things?" Dr. James asked.

"Yes," Benjamin said. "I make model train sets at home. I like doing that. I wish they would let me do it at school."

"Okay, good. Why don't you come show me how to build something with these blocks?"

Benjamin slid off the couch and onto the ground with Dr. James. Immediately he began assembling the wooden blocks to resemble a medieval castle he had seen in his history book at school.

"I'm using the triangles to make peaks and the cylinders to make columns," he said. "The bridges are rectangular. I'm going to make it tall, because one of the features of Gothic architecture is height, so—"

"Okay, Benjamin, I'm done with the blocks," said Dr. James, who had only made several small piles. He pulled an action figure from the basket of toys and handed it to Benjamin. "Let's play with this now."

Benjamin stared at the action figure. Why did Dr. James change the game? Benjamin wanted to keep building his castle. But Dr. James was starting to disassemble it—all of Benjamin's work crumbling!

"No!" Benjamin cried. "Stop it!" But it was too late. Benjamin's castle fell, triangles mixed with squares mixed with rectangles. "You ruined it!" Benjamin yelled, so consumed with frustration that he launched a fist directly at Dr. James's face. It grazed his jaw, and Dr. James made a sound that for a second startled Benjamin into silence. He stared at Dr. James, waiting to see what would happen next.

"That's enough for today, Benjamin," Dr. James said, rising to his feet. "Let's get your parents now."

. . .

Several weeks later, Jason said curtly, "We've done the six hours. Do you have any idea what's going on with him, or are we going to get yet another referral?"

Marie gave his knee a sharp squeeze.

Dr. James gave Jason an understanding nod. "When you first came here, there was some question on your part about the possibility of Benjamin being on the higher end of the autism spectrum; that was the focus of my work with you all. What I'd like to do now is first go over what we've done as far as the evaluation. Then I'll let you know what I think it means and what some next steps might be. Sound okay?

Jason, chagrined, nodded.

"That's perfect," Marie said.

"We managed to collect quite a bit of information over the past few weeks," Dr. James said, opening a folder. "I've reviewed all of Benjamin's records, completed parent and teacher interviews, conducted some individual testing and multiple behavioral observations, and have had parent and teacher behavior rating scales completed, including a rating scale specific to autism spectrum disorders. Now, after looking at all the assessment information together, I do think Benjamin meets the criteria for Asperger's disorder."

Dr. James paused, letting the words sink in. Jason felt a moment of instinctive denial, a heat in his chest, and Marie took a deep breath and let it out slowly.

"Okay," Dr. James said. "Asperger's disorder is on the autism spectrum and describes characteristics in a child, including significantly impaired social interaction—such as underdeveloped peer relationships and poor understanding and use of nonverbal cues—as well as restricted repetitive patterns of behavior. In your son's case, this would be his intense preoccupation with trains and fact-based subjects, as well as his resistance to transition and change. I know this is a lot to take in," he added, his voice softening. "What are you thinking about this?"

Jason voiced his reaction tentatively, realizing how little he knew about the subject. "I thought kids with an autism spectrum disorder can't talk."

Dr. James nodded. "One feature of autism spectrum disorders is an impairment in communication. It might be helpful for you to think of autism spectrum disorders as being on a continuum. Benjamin is on the higher-skilled and more verbal end. He has an excellent vocabulary and knowledge base in certain subjects, yet he is impaired in his ability to sustain a conversation and communicate to share experiences with others."

Quietly, her voice shaking slightly, Marie said, "I knew

it. I've been doing so much research, and it sounded so much like Benjamin. Now we know, and part of me is relieved, but another part of me is more worried than ever. What does this mean for his future? I mean, what you've described doesn't sound horrible, but I compare it to his behavior, and—" Throat choked, Marie couldn't continue.

Jason could feel tears pricking his eyes as he draped an arm over Marie's shoulders and brought her close. He didn't want to believe it, but everything Dr. James said about Asperger's sounded like Benjamin. His first thought was, *There's no cure.* His next was, *What do we do now?* He needed action, a plan.

"First, I recommend having him evaluated for a special education program at his school," Dr. James said. "You'll need to request an IEP team evaluation—IEP stands for Individualized Education Program. My evaluation should be forwarded to them, and I would ask that you make the referral due to a suspected special education need for students with autism."

Marie took feverish notes, numbering the steps to take.

"For additional help," Dr. James said, "I would call the county and talk to someone in the department of human services. They may be able to help with additional resources down the road if Benjamin needs them. I'm particularly concerned about the frequency and intensity of his meltdowns. Since the school police liaison officer has been called once, Benjamin is probably already on their radar, so to speak."

Marie's head was spinning. *Additional resources?* What did that even mean?

"In the meantime," Dr. James added, "I'd strongly recommend finding an individual therapist who can work with you and your son. The individual sessions should help you with behavior management strategies in the home. I would definitely try to find someone with experience working with higher skilled kids with autism spectrum disorders. I can get you some names to contact if you'd like to see if they have openings. You should also look into an after-school social skills group to help Benjamin in his interactions with others."

Marie nodded.

"The meltdowns, as I said, concern me," Dr. James said. "There are many people in the world with Asperger's disorder, and most are doing quite well. However, in Benjamin's case, if the emotional problems persist—particularly the aggression toward others—you may want to look into a consultation with a child and adolescent psychiatrist."

"This is a lot to take in," Marie said, looking at her notebook. Her handwriting was rushed and messy. "But thank you. You've been very helpful."

Marie and Jason were silent on the car ride home. Jason made decent money as an engineer, and Marie's retail salary helped, but already their income went quickly with a mortgage and three kids. How would they pay for all the services Benjamin might need? And what about college one day? Was that out of the question? Would Benjamin need special care and treatment all his life? What would happen to Benjamin when he and Marie were no longer around?

Marie internalized many of the same thoughts as they neared home. There was nothing worse than to hear her child had a disability, but she shoved the sharpness of that word aside and instead intently focused on what was next.

PART II
THE FIGHT

"Okay, Benjamin," Marie said in the car. "Remember what we talked about?"

"You want me to play with other kids like me," Benjamin said, looking out the window. "We are going to learn social and emotional skills."

Mom and Dad had been talking to him about the after-school social skills group for a month, ever since the last time they had seen the talking doctor. They told him that the class would teach him things he wasn't learning in school, things about interacting with other people and how to handle his anger. To Benjamin, this was all purely abstract. He recognized that he was different from other kids, but he didn't understand what he needed to learn and wasn't terribly interested in being as socially interactive as they were in the first place. Though he would like a friend, in theory, *things* and *ideas* were so much more interesting.

Mom pulled up in front of a low brick building with blue double doors.

"All right, we're here," Mom sang.

"I know we're here," Benjamin said. "You've parked the

car, and it's four twenty-eight. The after-school social skills group starts at four-thirty."

Mom didn't say anything, just opened her car door and then Benjamin's for him to get out. She tried to take his hand, but he pulled it away as they walked to the double doors.

There were seven other kids in the classroom, all boys. Three of them looked younger than Benjamin; the rest looked his age. There were five other moms, besides his mom, and one dad sitting at the back of the room, a good distance away from the kids. The kids were up front sitting in a semi-circle, and a woman stood before them, writing on a dry erase board.

"You must be Benjamin!" the teacher said. She came up and knelt in front of him. "It's nice to meet you, Benjamin. I'm Miss Andrea."

Benjamin looked at her and then at Mom, who was watching him, and then at the white tile floor.

"What do we say when someone says it's nice to meet you?" Mom prompted.

"I say 'it's nice to meet you' back to them," Benjamin mumbled.

"Well done!" the teacher said with eye contact and a big smile. She patted Mom on the arm and said, "That's a very good start. Why don't you come sit down with the other kids, Benjamin? Your mom will be with the rest of the parents."

Already, Benjamin didn't want to be there. It felt like more school. He followed Miss Andrea with reluctant, shuffling steps and sat down slightly apart from the semicircle. One boy elbowed another, nodding toward Benjamin. "Check it out. New kid's too good for us. Looks like a geek."

From the back of the room, a voice said, "Sean, that's enough." Benjamin turned to see a woman shaking her head. She looked at Benjamin's mom. "I'm sorry," she said in a lower voice that Benjamin could still hear. "He has oppositional defiant disorder. We have a lot of issues with bullying."

Mom's lips were pressed together. "This was what I was afraid of. We looked for a group specifically for Asperger's kids, but they were all full. He gets bullied enough at school—this is the last thing he needs."

"Well, this leads into our discussion for today," Miss Andrea said. "First, Benjamin, why don't you get a little closer to the rest of the group?"

"I really don't want to," Benjamin said, rocking slightly. "I don't want to be here, and I don't need to be here."

Miss Andrea sighed. "Okay, Benjamin. We're going to move on now and get started. We learn and practice different social skills in this group. The skill we'll be learning today is *apologizing to others*—telling others in a sincere way when we are sorry for doing something that created a problem. Like, for example," she added, looking at Sean, "saying something that hurts another person's feelings."

Miss Andrea reached behind the dry erase board and pulled out a poster. On top, it said, "Apologizing: Skill Steps." She ran through the list, first explaining how difficult apologizing could be. "Sometimes you don't realize you've done something wrong," she said. "Other times you do, but you feel fearful or anxious at the idea of apologizing. That's why it's helpful to practice this skill."

Benjamin was not at all interested in the discussion. He looked at the floor, pressing his nail into the hairline grooves between the tiles. He started counting the number of tiles between where he sat and the front wall: exactly nine squares in a straight line. He counted the number of tiles between the left wall and the right wall: twelve. He tried to do the math in his head.

Time passed, and Miss Andrea was still talking about apologizing. She ran through scenarios: accidentally knocking someone's notebook off her desk, saying something mean to a friend, being late for school, lying to your parents. Benjamin had done some of the things she mentioned, but he couldn't remember ever apologizing. How was he supposed to know when he'd done something that created a problem? He couldn't tell what people were feeling or thinking. Trying to wrap his mind around it made Benjamin want to go home.

Miss Andrea said, "Okay, kids, let's break into groups of four for role play. Benjamin, we're going to act out some scenarios that require an apology, and then we'll talk as a group about how it went. Don't worry," she added with a smile, "I'll help you."

"No fair," Sean said. Then under his breath he sneered at Benjamin, "Teacher's pet."

Benjamin was uncomfortable. What had he done to make Sean not like him?

The rest of class was slow and painful. Sean and Benjamin were in the same group, and they were supposed to "act out" scenarios that were written on cards. Benjamin didn't know how to be anyone but himself, or in any situation other than the one he was in, so he hardly said anything, and Sean made comments about him when Miss Andrea was with the other group. When it was over, Miss Andrea gave Benjamin a sticker that said "Solid Effort!" and a small piece of candy—a mint. The other kids in his group—including Sean—got stickers that said "Super Effort!" and their choice of three miniature candy bars. Benjamin felt like crying. He wanted a sticker that said "Super Effort!" He wanted to choose his candy! Feverishly, he ripped up the sticker and threw the pieces on the ground.

"I hate this place!" he yelled. "I deserve the same candy they got—I tried super, too! I want to go home right now and never come back!"

Mom rushed to the front of the room and took him by the arm. Benjamin shook her off, and she collected the shreds of sticker from the floor. "I'm sorry," she said to Miss Andrea. "I'm going to take him home, or this will just get worse. Hopefully he'll do better next week. Benjamin, let's go."

Benjamin hardly heard her over his anger. He ran ahead of her out the door and toward their car. He would have kept running if Mom hadn't caught up to him and grabbed his hand, holding him in place while he yelled.

"This was stupid! *You're* stupid! Why did you have to bring me here? I never want to come back!"

"Come on, Benjamin." Mom held his arms as she opened the car door and pushed him inside, where Benjamin collapsed on the seat. He lashed out with his fists when Mom reached around him for the seatbelt, but she managed to buckle it around him. He snapped it out of place as soon as she closed the door and spent the ride home hitting the back of Mom's seat and yelling that he wanted to get out and would blow up the car if she didn't stop and open the doors *right now*! By the time they pulled into the driveway, Benjamin was drained and walked straight to his bedroom, shutting the door behind him.

Summer came, and Mom kept taking him to the class once a week. He never grew to like it. The only thing he liked was getting "Super Effort!" stickers, but getting anything else immediately sent him into a rage. At home, he spent a lot of time with his train sets and in the living room, watching the History Channel and reading science textbooks. By the time he started fifth grade, he'd learned a lot about history. He thought he could use it to start conversation, the way Miss Andrea talked about, and make new friends.

"In 1974, a Japanese soldier named Hiroo Onoda came out of the jungle in a place called Lubang," Benjamin told the girl sitting next to him. It was something he'd just read yesterday. "He was hiding there for twenty-nine years."

The girl—a redhead with a ponytail—looked at him and then the boy at her right. "Um," she said, "Okay."

"He did not know his country had surrendered."

The girl gave him another glance, but Benjamin couldn't read her expression.

"Benjamin," said his teacher. "Please be quiet while I'm explaining what we're doing today."

By lunchtime, Benjamin was branded—again—as a loser. Before he started social skills, Mom and Dad had told him he had Asperger's disorder. Mom said it meant he learned differently from other kids—that he saw the world from a unique perspective. He wondered how other people saw the world. To him, it was a lot of people asking things of him that didn't make sense and weren't interesting or important. Most often, he just wished to be left alone. With his train sets and encyclopedias, he didn't feel "different." He felt happy. These things relaxed him, reduced his feelings of anxiety. They *made sense*—unlike people.

But at school, the teachers didn't let him look at encyclopedias, and there were definitely no train sets, and he didn't feel happy. He felt like running away.

So, one day, he did. When the teacher told him to go to the bathroom, even though he didn't need to, and everybody laughed, he ran down the hallway and out the front doors of the school. He ran past the cars that were still dropping kids off and out the gates, as if he were going home, but instead he turned left, following the map in his mind through a bunch of trees—he imagined like the jungle Hiroo Onoda had hidden in—and he pushed through them until he reached the train tracks. He rocked back and forth in the shade for what seemed like hours, waiting for a train to pass. He heard the whistle long before the ground shivered beneath him, and finally from around a bend hurtled an orange and black Burlington locomotive. Benjamin sat close enough to the tracks to feel the heat from the train as it roared past, and he beamed at the *thu-thunk, thu-thunk* of the train on the rails. The sound made him feel grounded, steady and safe right where he was. He lost all track of time, waiting for train after train to roll by. After the trains stopped, he just looked at leaves and bugs, comparing them to what he'd seen in his science books and trying to figure out what they were.

Long after dark, he made his way home. Blue and red lights flashed as he turned into his neighborhood, and he was startled to see police cars in the driveway. Why were the police there?

The house exploded in noise as soon as Benjamin walked through the door. Mom jumped off the couch and ran to him, and Dad bolted over from where he was talking to two officers.

"Benjamin!" Mom cried, grabbing him. "Where have you been? Are you okay? You *ran away from school*? Don't you *ever* do that again, do you hear me?"

Mom was crying, and Benjamin writhed away from her grasp. "Stop touching me, I'm home now," he said.

"Damn it, Benjamin," Dad said. "What were you thinking? You scared us to death!"

Benjamin looked at Mom and Dad, who were clearly alive, and then at the police. "Why are the police here? They come for crimes and things," he added.

Mom wiped her face and looked at the officers. "Thank you for coming. Can I please get a copy of the incident report?"

...

"I understand your concerns," said Mrs. Barrett, Benjamin's school principal. "But I can assure you that your son is safe here."

"How can you tell me that my child is safe?" Marie said incredulously. "He *ran away* from school grounds. He could have been killed!"

"Ma'am, with all due respect, your son was supposed to go to the bathroom. We can't be with him one hundred percent of the time."

"That's actually something I'd like to talk to you about," Marie said. "In the paperwork for the IEP team evaluation that found him to qualify for services for autism, I saw something about the Individuals with Disabilities Education Act."

"IDEA," Mrs. Barrett said, nodding. "Yes."

"I've done more research, and under IDEA, every child has a right to a free and appropriate education. The IEP for each child needs to ensure that each child is able to benefit from his education. With all of these issues, Benjamin isn't benefiting. He needs more help. We want to reconvene the IEP team and get a one-to-one aide for him."

"A one-to-one aide is pretty extreme," Mrs. Barrett said, jotting down a note. "We're certainly happy to reconvene, but I have to tell you that there are other options we'll probably look at before considering a one-to-one."

Marie felt a flash of heat—she'd been getting those lately, quick rushes that made her sweat in moments of frustration. She took a deep breath. "Let's please just schedule the meeting. We'll discuss everything then."

The following week, Marie and Jason met with Mrs. Barrett, Benjamin's teacher Mrs. Atkinson, and Benjamin's special education teacher and school psychologist. Marie and Jason had also invited Dr. James. They met at seven-thirty, before school began, in a small conference room. The purpose of the meeting was to talk about what "special education services and supports" were necessary for Benjamin to benefit from his program. Marie and Jason had agreed before the meeting: they would not accept anything but a one-to-one aide. They believed it was what Benjamin needed if he had any hope of academic success—someone to help keep him focused, support him in completing his schoolwork, and work with him when he was agitated. They would do everything they needed in order to achieve their goal.

The meeting went much the way Mrs. Barrett had told Marie it would—the district first wanted to do a new functional behavior assessment on Benjamin, creating a new behavior support plan before trying a one-to-one aide. Marie opened her binder, pushing it across the conference table to Mrs. Barrett and Mrs. Atkinson.

"Look, I know your funding is probably limited," Marie said, "and what we're asking for costs money. But please, just look through this binder. It's obvious that Benjamin needs the one-on-one support, and I don't want to waste time on more assessments and more plans before eventually arriving here anyway."

"If I may interject," Dr. James said, "I'd like to remind the district that Benjamin has a history of sensory integration disorder, ADHD, and now Asperger's disorder with co-existing significant emotional and behavior outbursts. Previous interventions have not proven effective. I believe that extra adult support is necessary for Benjamin to learn in school—and to manage his behavior as it presents any issues. To be frank, the frequency, duration, and intensity of Benjamin's educational and social behavioral needs warrant a one-to-one aide."

While Marie was grateful to have Dr. James on their side, she couldn't help feeling overwhelmed at his description. Was this really their son he was talking about? The sweet, quiet infant she had cuddled in the hospital and then brought home, awash with joy?

"It's true that Benjamin is often extremely disruptive in class," Mrs. Atkinson said, interrupting Marie's thoughts. "From my perspective, it's nearly impossible to keep him on task while also teaching and supervising the other students." She looked at Mrs. Barrett. "A one-to-one aide might be beneficial to everyone involved."

Marie and Jason exchanged glances. This seemed promising.

"We'll give this careful review," Mrs. Barrett said. "Thank you both for coming in."

In the end, it took six weeks of ongoing discussions with the district—*after* trying a new, unsuccessful behavior intervention plan for three months—for them to agree to provide Benjamin with a one-to-one aide. They had an exhaustive checklist of requirements, each of which necessitated proof. Marie found every instance she'd recorded or report she'd been given of Benjamin 's behavioral problems, including incidents of self-injury—such as when he punched through the window or banged his head on the floor—or injury to others. She provided the district with his evaluations that showed diagnoses of a sensory integration disorder, ADHD, and Asperger's, and showed them occupational therapy reports and a write-up on the after-school social skills group. She had notes on previous report cards about Benjamin's difficulties staying on task, as well as his poor social skills, lack of friends, and other problematic social interactions. The district fought her at most every turn, suggesting alternatives such as finding him a peer buddy, adding him to the school psychologist's regular caseload, and adding a half hour of school social work per week. Eventually, however, persistence and knowledge of Benjamin's rights—as well as the frequency, severity, duration, and intensity of his behavior—showed he *needed* a one-to-one aide to benefit from his special education. An aide was procured for him, and she would begin working with him the next month.

Marie kept a careful log of the experience and added it to her binder of Benjamin's medical history and other evaluations. She had swiftly learned that to make any strides in care for him, they needed proof, proof, proof. Well, let anyone fire any question they wanted at her; she had everything recorded and neatly organized. The paperwork included results from physicals, school academics and IQ score, notes and recommendations from his pediatrician, occupational therapist, and psychologist, any X-rays for breaks and sprains, and even records from his last TB test and eye exam.

The one-to-one aide was a victory, but dealing with Benjamin was another story. How were they supposed to teach him consequences for his actions if he didn't understand the relationship between his behavior and consequences? Benjamin's impulsivity was worsening as he got older. He obviously had great difficulty with organizational skills, considering the likely outcomes of his behavior, identifying what was bothering him, managing frustration, moving off an original idea, transitioning from an activity, and appreciating how his behavior affected others. He didn't seem to realize that punching through a window could result in scraped and broken knuckles, nor did he think running away might lead to getting lost or kidnapped or hit by a car. He didn't see that throwing books and vases across the room might lead to giving his brother or sister a black eye. And he didn't recognize that the things he said could hurt others' feelings.

"I hate you! You always blame me!" was what he commonly screamed at Marie when he was angry.

He swore at Jason, using ugly four-letter words. Once, in a fit of anger when Jason tried to punish him at home for hitting his aide, Benjamin screamed, "I'll kill you, you just wait!"

Zach was scared of his older brother and slept with Marie and Jason. If Mandy was home, she was in her room with the door locked. But most days, she stayed at friends' houses as long as she could. Jason did what he could when he was at home, but he often worked late. He felt pressured to make as much money as possible for Benjamin's care. He also secretly liked being out of the house. When Marie looked at herself in the mirror, she was shocked at the growing streaks of gray in her dark hair, the puffiness of her eyes, and sad lines around her mouth. She was only forty but looked ten years older.

Four years after Benjamin was first prescribed Ritalin—and after consistent six-month dosage adjustments—Marie and Jason recognized that the medication was no longer helping Benjamin. It was supposed to help with attention, hyperactivity, and impulsivity, and it *had* at first, but now his meltdowns—zero to sixty with seemingly no provocation—made it undeniable that he needed something else. Benjamin's doctor recommended a medication called Strattera, so—still with heavy hearts—Marie and Jason started him on the pill. They began at the lowest therapeutic dosage, ten milligrams, taken with breakfast—though Benjamin's doctor had recommended they go higher—and hoped for the best.

• • •

Benjamin was starting to feel funny. He was nauseated and didn't want to eat, and his moods were up and down. He didn't feel like himself. It was as if he were trapped inside another thing's body and needed to cut his way out. The problem was that he *couldn't* cut his way out. He'd need to cut his way *in*.

It was art time during school, and the students were working on a project about the Mayans. They were supposed to create masks by cutting geometric shapes out of construction paper, outlining the shapes with black paint, and then using one set of complementary colors to fill in the masks. Benjamin chose shades of blue and brown and lined up the little pots of paint on his desk from lightest to darkest color. The scissors were on the far right and the construction paper directly in front of him.

Benjamin tried to focus, but his head felt foggy, as if he were trying to see through cellophane. The boy to his right whispered, "Watch this," to the girl next him. Before Benjamin realized what was happening, the boy darted his hand to Benjamin's desk and stole a pot of paint. Just like that, dynamite exploded in Benjamin's chest.

"AHHHHH!" he screamed, shoving the boy. The chair tipped over, and the boy fell to the ground, hitting his head on the leg of the desk behind them. "THAT'S MY PAINT!"

The classroom erupted with noise, scaring Benjamin, but he was too focused on the paint and the dynamite feeling to close his ears. His aide tried to grab him, forcing his arms to his sides, but he slammed his head into her chest and pushed away from her. He saw the pot of paint on the ground, where the boy was yelling and crying, and grabbed it, and then the glint of scissors on his desk caught Benjamin's eye. He wanted to be out of his skin. He grabbed the scissors to a chorus of "Benjamin, no!" and gave himself one long slice down his left arm. They were kids' scissors with dull blades, but Benjamin pressed hard enough to break his skin, and bright blood pooled to the surface. Benjamin watched it in fascination, but he still felt trapped. He was going for another cut when the kid who had stolen Benjamin's paint brushed his ankle, and Benjamin instinctively bent and speared the boy's hand with the scissors. He felt the rubbery resistance of skin before the pressure broke and the blade cut through.

The boy howled, grabbing his hand. "He stabbed me! I'm bleeding!"

Benjamin stared at him, shaking, and then the teacher and a security guard grabbed him. Benjamin thrashed and yelled, and by the time they got to the nurse's office, Benjamin was not even Benjamin anymore. He didn't feel or hear himself. He couldn't breathe. He kept gasping for air, but the more he sucked in through his mouth, the less seemed to go into his body, because he still needed more air and more air.

"What's happening to him?" a male voice asked.

"He's hyperventilating," the nurse said.

Suddenly a brown paper bag was in front of Benjamin's face, and he pawed it away, tearing a hole in it. The nurse quickly grabbed another bag from a drawer.

"It'll help you breathe!" the nurse said loudly. "Just breathe into it."

Benjamin was crying and breathless and too desperate to fight anymore, so he breathed into the paper bag, blowing it up, and then sucked the air back in. The paper bag made a dry slapping noise, and slowly, slowly his heart wasn't hitting his chest so hard, and sounds started coming back, and Benjamin's arm hurt, and he still felt trapped.

· · ·

Marie must have run three reds on the way to Benjamin's school. When she arrived, Benjamin was in the nurse's office, still in the throes of a full-on meltdown.

"I don't know what to do with him!" the nurse said over Benjamin's cries. "He's torn this office up, and the police are on their way."

"The police?" Marie crossed the office to where Benjamin was now in a corner, rocking and wailing. "Look at him," she said. "Does it look like he meant to hurt anybody?"

"He stabbed a boy in the hand," said the nurse.

Benjamin looked up at Marie with a flushed, blotchy face, his eyes small and red from crying, and rocked harder. "I don't want to be in my skin," he said.

Marie tried not to cry. "We're going to take you to the doctor, okay? We'll help you feel better."

Mrs. Barrett joined them in the room. Her face was harried. "The other boy's parents are on their way," she said. "I'm sure they'll want to speak with you."

"I'm sure they will, but I need to get my son to the hospital. Just have them call me."

Jason met Marie at the hospital, where the cut on Benjamin's arm was cleaned and bandaged and they gave permission for Benjamin to be given a light sedative. In the children's psychiatry ward, they watched their son breathe peacefully in bed.

"He's worse," Jason said.

"I know," Marie replied.

A police officer arrived soon after to take a statement. He recorded Benjamin's age, height, and weight, and Marie and Jason told him about Benjamin's mental health and special education history, SID, ADHD, and Asperger's diagnoses.

"Are the other parents pressing charges?" Marie asked, reaching for Jason's hand.

"They're considering it. Your son hurt the other kid pretty bad." The cop glanced over his paperwork. "This isn't the first time we've been called for Benjamin, I see.

Look, my advice is get control over your kid fast, or he's going to end up in juvenile corrections someday."

Jason's face flushed, and Marie quickly jumped in before he could fire back a retort. "We're doing our best," she said.

Since Benjamin had hurt someone else and himself *and* was on medication *and* had warranted police attention, the hospital wanted to keep him at an in-patient psychiatric unit for the next five days. While it was difficult to determine how much of Benjamin's behavior was due to Asperger's disorder, doctors immediately keyed into the fact that Benjamin was taking Strattera, after which his moods became more unpredictable and aggression heightened. That, coupled with Benjamin's new behavior of trying to hurt himself, led them to believe he was experiencing side effects of the medication. Marie was so upset she had to leave the room.

A week later, she was back in Mrs. Barrett's office.

"As I told you over the phone, we've done everything we can to meet Benjamin's education needs, but we're almost out of options." Mrs. Barrett sighed. "You're lucky the other parents decided not to press charges. I have a strong feeling there's something more going on here. After all, we have other kids here with Asperger's disorder and while they can have their moments, they are not as explosive as Benjamin. Perhaps you should take him for another evaluation."

Marie laughed harshly and pulled out the three-ring binder from her bag. She dropped it on Mrs. Barrett's desk. "Remember this? I've taken him for every kind of evaluation," she said. "So, what are you telling me? You're just kicking Benjamin out of school?"

"Not at all," Mrs. Barrett said. "We're committed to Benjamin's education. While we determine what the right next moves are, I'm recommending a school district program called Homebound Instruction."

"What's that?" Marie asked warily.

"In Homebound Instruction, a special education teacher will meet with Benjamin for two hours twice a week, either at your home or in a public area."

Marie stared at Mrs. Barrett. "That's it? Two hours, twice a week? That's hardly an appropriate education! He's in special education and has a disability, remember?"

"As I said, it's a temporary solution," Mrs. Barrett said hurriedly. "Just two months, while we figure out the next plan of action to help your son."

Marie closed her eyes. She was exhausted. "All right," she said. "That's fine."

Just two months. What Mrs. Barrett failed to take into account was that Marie would need to quit her job in order to make Homebound Instruction work. After all, what would Benjamin do for the rest of the week? He still needed an education, and now it seemed as though Marie was his only option.

Marie decided to use the Homebound Instruction for the four hours a week and to home school Benjamin the rest of the time. Home schooling her son was the hardest thing Marie had ever done. This classroom of one was consuming her life.

The day started at six, when she and Jason woke up. Half asleep and almost without saying a word to each other, they showered and dressed for the day. Jason left first, taking four-year-old Zach to childcare. At first, Zach hated it. "How come Benjamin gets to stay home with you?" he asked Marie. "You love him more than me!" Marie's heart broke at the wounded accusation.

Mandy, now twelve, was largely independent. She rose at seven and ate a quick breakfast, usually cereal, in the kitchen before her bus arrived. "Bye, guys!" she called, giving a quick wave as she ran out the door.

Then it was just Marie and Benjamin. She usually tried to reserve ten minutes to herself before waking him at eight. Often, she thought those precious minutes, sitting at the kitchen table with her coffee and a newspaper, saved her sanity.

She woke Benjamin with a cheerful but firm "Rise and shine, Benjamin-boy." He usually awoke without difficulty, and Marie reminded him to make his bed. If he was in one of his Benjamin-moods, he refused. That was when Marie knew it would be a long day. Otherwise, he obediently circled the bed, haphazardly tucking sheet corners and tossing pillows. Next came breakfast. At the advice of different doctors and nutritionists, Marie had tried varying his meals, but breakfast was the one Benjamin refused to adjust. Guiltily, for the sake of starting the day with ease, Marie still made him his French toast, which she arranged on his train plate. When he finished eating, Marie said, "You know what comes next, Benjamin."

"After breakfast, we wash our dishes," Benjamin intoned. "I know, I know."

He took his train plate to the sink, washed it, and then slid it into the dish rack to dry.

"Let's sit down and go over our lesson plans for the day," Marie said.

They went into the living room, where Benjamin now had a small desk, and Marie gave a brief summary of what they would cover in school today. The only subject he enjoyed was history, and he pored over the textbook with one hundred percent focus. If Benjamin read something once—something he *wanted* to read—he never forgot it. It wasn't unusual for Benjamin to quote his history book two months after the original lesson. In these moments, Marie saw how truly bright and special her son was. But the rest of the day was nothing short of war. He said over and over again how boring the material was, and he hated switching from one subject to the next. Worst of all were reading and writing. Marie wasn't sure if he just wasn't interested or if the concepts were truly abstract to him, but he completely shut down when it was time to read passages or work on grammar. His first recourse was to completely ignore Marie, which drove her insane.

"Benjamin." She leaned in close to him and put her index and middle finger close to his eyes, which were looking over her right shoulder. "Benjamin, it's time to focus. Look at me." She drew her fingers to her own eyes, and Benjamin looked at her for several seconds. Marie felt a combination of overwhelming love and sadness when she stared into his eyes. She wanted nothing more than to connect with her son, but he seemed inaccessible to her. After initial attempts to reinforce his behavior and motivate him failed, Marie tried using punishment. Marie usually avoided negative consequences with Benjamin, as they tended not to be very effective and sometimes resulted in explosive behavior, but one day she was at her wits' end.

"Benjamin, you know the rules and how our day works. It is important for your learning that we finish every subject. If we don't finish this reading assignment today, there's not going to be any playing with trains tonight. I'm serious."

The prospect of losing train privileges sent Benjamin into a full-on meltdown. He was lanky but tall for his age, swiftly gaining on Marie's slight five feet two inches, and he was no longer easy to physically control when he flew into a rage. He grabbed his textbook and threw it at the wall, screaming, "I hate you! I hate you! You always blame me!"

"Benjamin, you know that isn't true," Marie said, trying to keep her voice calm. "We love you."

"No, you don't! You blame me, and I hate you!" He swept the contents of his desk to the floor, where a glass shattered and spilled sweet tea all over the hard wood. He was wired and tense, his face red and pinched in anger.

"Calm down, Benjamin." Marie circled around him, trying to get to a place where she could hold his arms at his sides. Meltdowns that started like this never ended well. "Can't you see that you're acting unreasonably?"

Benjamin glared at her. Right when he was reaching for another textbook, Marie darted forward and wrapped her arms around him from behind. Sometimes, if she held him tightly enough, he calmed down. Once, she actually had to sit on him to keep him restrained, and she cried for half an hour afterwards for shame. Another time, Benjamin shoved right past her, knocking her into the coffee table and scraping her shin, and bolted out the front door.

"Benjamin!" Marie yelled, limping after him. "Get back here!"

She chased him barefoot for two blocks before finally managing to catch him and drag him home. He screamed and cried the whole way, pitching himself in all directions to escape Marie's grasp. While she held onto her son as hard as she could, he yelled obscenities Marie didn't even know he knew. Before she wrangled him through the front door, he landed one punch in her gut that knocked her air out and another on her mouth, cutting her lip. Now she always wore tennis shoes at home, and she and Jason installed a lock on the front door that was out of Benjamin's reach.

On other days, the ones that weren't so bad, Benjamin was generally subdued and mildly irritable, but nothing major. "This school work is boring." His little face was pale and drawn as he looked out the window. "I want to learn and read more about science and history. Why can't we learn about chemistry symbols or the Bubonic plague–something cool, for once? Or at least be around other people."

Marie looked online and found that there was a homeschooling community in their part of the city. Excited and energized, she joined the message board and email list and took Benjamin on a bowling outing to meet homeschooled kids his age. At the bowling alley, Marie's heart ached when she saw him try to make friends. He wasn't good at two-way conversations, so he talked at the kids about how good of a bowler he was until they invariably walked away. Some of the home-schooled boys said cruel things to Benjamin, calling him a geek and making him cry. Still, when it was just the two of them at home, he said, "I want to be with the other kids and show them the right way to set up model trains."

At four o'clock, Marie had to pick Zach up from childcare. By then she was exhausted. Mandy arrived home at four-thirty, letting herself in, and helped Marie by pulling out the ingredients they'd need to cook dinner. (Marie tacked a menu for each week up on the fridge.) Cooking together was their ritual, but the time was always interrupted by some minor catastrophe: Benjamin hitting Zach, Zach throwing his own normal four-year-old tantrum, a phone call from Jason saying he'd be late. *God help me,* Marie thought during those times, and she forced herself through the rest of the evening with more willpower than she'd ever known she had. By the time all three kids were in bed, Marie usually couldn't remember one real conversation she'd had with Mandy or Jason that day, nor her last uninterrupted half hour to cuddle and read with Zach. She was losing herself to Benjamin.

"I'm done," she told Jason one night, nearly two months in. They were in the backyard, one on each swing, pushing themselves lightly in the night air. Without expecting to, she broke down and wept. "I can't do this anymore."

Jason let out a long, shaking sigh. "I know. I'm sorry you've had to do it pretty much on your own."

"I think we need to go back to the school district," Marie said. "They're obligated to help us. It's not right that we're on our own."

"I agree," Jason said. "I'll help however you need me to."

Marie called Mrs. Barrett the next day to set up an appointment.

"I'm so sorry," Mrs. Barrett said the following week. "I understand the frustration you must be feeling. But we've recognized that outside of Homebound Instruction, there's nothing more we can do for him here. And our district does not have any alternative settings or schools that would meet his needs. I think it's time you begin looking into an alternative education out of district."

The district special education director was also in the room, and she leaned forward to give Marie a sympathetic pat on the arm. "There are a lot of wonderful options out there," she said, "and we'll help provide recommendations."

Marie looked at Jason, who sat beside her. They were prepared for this answer. "We think you're right about alternative education—but that's something for the district to provide."

Mrs. Barrett was silent for a moment. "I'll be honest with you. We've had numerous budget cuts, and funding for all programs is extremely limited—"

Marie cut her off. "Funding, yes, I know. I sympathize, but that doesn't change the fact that you're legally obligated to ensure that Benjamin has access to special education services and supports—I read that in the IDEA literature."

Jason took one of Marie's hands, stilling her. "Look," he said, keeping his voice calm, "we've reached out to a special education advocate and attorney, just in case. If we can't come to an agreement here, he'll be in touch with the district directly."

"It's not necessary to consult with an attorney," Mrs. Barrett protested, though she didn't seem entirely surprised.

"Believe me, this is the last thing we want," Marie said. "But under IDEA, parents have rights. And so does our son."

"What exactly do you want?" Mrs. Barrett said. "I want to support you however I can—tell me, and I'll take it to the board."

What exactly do I want? Marie thought. She wanted Benjamin to not need medication with side effects such as "suicidal ideation," mood swings, panic attacks, and aggression toward others. She wanted him to stop coming home from school in tears after being teased and bullied. She wanted the meltdowns, the rages, to stop. She wanted to sleep at night without worrying that her ten-year-old child was going walk out of the house—or worse. She wanted her other two children to feel safe and get the attention and love they deserved; she wanted them to feel that they mattered. She wanted to stop patching holes in the walls and replacing windows. She wanted things with Jason to be like before they were married, when they went out to dinner and saw their friends and *kissed*. She wanted to stop being imprisoned. She wanted normalcy.

Marie was crying, struggling to express her feelings in a professional way. "We only want what Benjamin is entitled to—a free and appropriate education," she managed. "We think he needs to go somewhere safe. Somewhere he can get the help he needs from people who work with children like him all the time and actually know what to do, because God knows we don't. In his case, as hard as it is for us, we think that means a therapeutic residential school." Marie paused, taking a shaky breath. "We need help, Mrs. Barrett. We really do. And we're not giving up until we find it."

PART III
THE FUTURE

It turned out that a follow-up letter from the advocate lawyer about IDEA and the mention of Benjamin's safety was the recipe for getting the district's attention—and cooperation, although it took six months. Six months in which the police were called three more times, and Marie nearly lost her mind trying to home school him. Six months in which Benjamin was diagnosed with a co-existing mood disorder—which the psychiatrist thought best accounted for his meltdowns, emotional regulation problems, low frustration tolerance, and how he at times didn't even remember being upset and felt so badly after—and was put back on Ritalin, a stimulant medication, and Abilify, a medication that crossed the blood-brain barrier to act directly on the central nervous system to affect brain function. Six months in which Child Protective Services had come to the home after being called by Zach's school to assess Zach, who had several times gone to school with bruises and once a black eye after being hit by Benjamin. And six months in which Mandy had moved in with Marie's parents at her own insistence. It was the most difficult six months they had ever experienced with

Benjamin, but finally—*finally*—they had secured funding for him at Genesee Lake School, a leading residential school for children and teens with special needs. After a few phone calls with the admissions department and a tour of the grounds, Marie and Jason felt it was the right place for Benjamin. Based on an admissions assessment, the school agreed. Now the day had arrived to drop him off.

Marie fought tears in the passenger seat as they neared the facilities. She glanced back at Benjamin, now eleven and often withdrawn and quiet when he wasn't agitated, preferring to read his books and use the computer. Every part of her knew this was the right choice—the only choice—to make for Benjamin, but she couldn't help feeling like a failure. She hadn't been able to help her son, and now she was leaving him in the care of strangers. Benjamin's clinical coordinator, whom she had met on the tour, had explained that the average length of placement varied depending on the child's progress and ability of the family and home school to provide a safe and supportive environment. Some kids stayed four to six months, while others stayed eighteen months or longer. In Benjamin's case, twelve to fifteen months might be appropriate.

On one hand, Marie couldn't imagine being away from her son for that long. On the other, she couldn't quite believe Benjamin would improve enough in that time to come home. She also felt a guilty sense of relief at the thought of twelve to fifteen months without the daily disasters that came with Benjamin. Poor Mandy and Zach would finally have two parents who could focus on them, and maybe Marie and Jason could also devote time to themselves—and each other—for a change.

Jason, too, felt anxious, guilty, and angry as he pulled up to Genesee Lake School. He was a man, after all, and men were supposed to take care of their families. But he had to rely on strangers to take care of his kid, and his family was falling apart. This felt like the last stop on a long journey—but what if it, like everything else they'd tried, failed? Then what would they do with Benjamin? What would happen to him?

"Okay, son, we're here," Jason said, trying to sound cheerful.

"Remember what we talked about," Marie added as they got out of the car. "This is *not* a punishment of any kind. You're here to learn skills that we can't teach you, so that you can be more independent later down the line."

Benjamin walked with them casually, as if this were any other day. "I can be more independent. That's not a big deal. I don't want to be here, though."

The campus was beautiful, a mix of historical and modern buildings surrounded by large, stunning trees and bordered by Genesee Lake. Though they had been there before, Marie was still struck by how well maintained the grounds were. That comforted her somehow, as it felt like a direct reflection of how well they would care for Benjamin.

As they neared the entrance, two staff members walked out with four children around Benjamin's age. One of the kids smiled at him. "Hi, we're going to the zoo today! Going to go see some little chimpanzees," he said.

"I like the zoo," Benjamin said. "My favorite animal is the African elephant. It's the heaviest mammal on land. It weighs up to fourteen thousand pounds and eats up to six hundred pounds of food a day. It—"

"Okay, Benjamin," Marie interrupted with a laugh. "Let's let these guys go to the zoo now."

Benjamin quieted, though his eyes flashed with hurt.

Inside, they met with Melanie, Benjamin's clinical co-ordinator, and Jake, the group supervisor. Melanie was in her mid-thirties, with a bright smile and reassuring manner. She would be Marie and Jason's main point of contact throughout Benjamin's stay at the Genesee Lake School, as well as offer counseling and family sessions. Jake was tall and lanky, dressed in khaki slacks and a button-down shirt.

"Okay, Benjamin, it's nice to meet you," Melanie said. "I'm going to have Jake walk you around, show you your room and our school. Does that sound all right?"

Benjamin bounced lightly on the balls of his feet, and Marie cringed. This was how a lot of his meltdowns started. Jason looked equally stressed, clenching his jaw, but Benjamin simply walked out with Jake. Marie sighed with relief.

For the next hour and a half, Melanie walked Jason and Marie through what they could expect from the com-ing months. On a previous visit, they'd gone through a thick admissions packet, Marie's hand cramping with the amount of times she signed her name on consent and release forms. She'd fought tears the whole time. It was as if she were giving away her child—and doing it by choice.

Now, seeming to read Marie's mind, Melanie said, "I want you both to know that yes, you signed a lot of paper-work, but you still have full guardianship over Benjamin. You have complete say in all of his treatment, including medication, and you can revoke that treatment at any time."

Marie's eyes stung with familiar tears. She pulled a

tissue from her purse as Melanie leaned across the table and looked her in the eyes. "You're still Benjamin's parents, okay? You're doing the right thing for him. We believe we have so much to offer him here, but look—no one stays forever. Our goal is to have him home as soon as he is ready."

Marie nodded, swallowing hard. "How often should we come visit?"

"Once every week or two is ideal," Melanie said. "Benjamin is your son, and it's important for him to see his family. For the first few weeks he's here, he will probably want to talk to you on the phone a lot. If you can speak to him every night or every other night, and show him that you're still his family and still supporting him, that will help his adjustment here and eventual transition home."

After Marie and Jason had answered questions about Benjamin's interests, preferred activities, and personal strengths and challenges, it was time to say goodbye. Melanie walked them through the residential area until they reached Benjamin's room. The walls were painted a soothing gray-blue, and a window by the single bed overlooked lush treed grounds. Benjamin was sitting at a small wooden desk, absorbed in a book.

"What's that book you're reading, Benjamin?" Jason asked.

Benjamin didn't look up.

"Benjamin," Jake said, "why don't you show your dad the cool book we found in the library?"

"*The History of Railroads and Canals in the United States,*" Benjamin mumbled.

Jason and Marie both gave laughs that were choked with tears.

They lingered for a while longer, commenting on how nice the room and view were, before finally recognizing they couldn't delay any longer.

"Honey," Marie said, approaching Benjamin. "It's time for Dad and me to leave. We'll be back to visit next Saturday, okay? In the meantime, you can call us anytime you want, and we'll give you a call tomorrow to see how you're doing."

Marie stood awkwardly by Benjamin's chair. He was so focused on the book that he hardly registered hearing her. All he said was, "Okay, Mom and Dad. I'll be all right. You can go now."

Marie looked at Jason. After all this time, all the years of struggle and months of battle to get him here, this casual farewell was somehow worse than if he had screamed and cried. Quickly—because Benjamin only tolerated quick hugs—they both hugged and kissed him.

"I love you, Benjamin," Marie said. She watched his eyes rove left to right on the book.

"I love you, too, kiddo," Jason said.

Benjamin looked up. "I love you both, too."

Jason took Marie's hand, and Melanie walked them out of the residential school. "I know that was hard for you both," she said, "but you did a great job during a difficult time. I'll call you tomorrow afternoon with an update on how Benjamin is doing. Call me anytime you need."

. . .

That night, Melanie sat with Benjamin in the back of the group room. While some kids watched TV, she went over the daily routine with him. She told him that the kids woke up at seven-fifteen, completed their shower and morning routine, ate breakfast at eight-fifteen, and then went to school on-grounds from nine to two forty-five. After school, the kids went to the group and dormitory areas and participated in different activities—including group and community outings and physical exercise—before and after dinner, and then there would be free time before bed. Melanie also showed him the group expectations that were posted on the wall—Respect, Responsibility, and Safety—and the visual schedule on his bedroom wall outlining all parts of the daily routine.

"We believe that understanding adult expectations and why they are important, as well as having structure and a predictable routine, are important for all of our kids," Melanie said. "Actually, these things are important for all of us in life. Let me ask you a question, Benjamin. Is it important for you to know what to expect during the day?"

Benjamin nodded. "It makes me nervous when I don't know what's coming next." After a beat, he added, almost defiantly, "Also, at home I eat French toast for breakfast every day. That's my routine, and that's the way I like it."

"We have French toast here," Melanie said. "But not every day. And we have other things, too."

The next day was Monday, and Benjamin woke up at seven thirty feeling anxious and displaced.

"Good morning, Benjamin," said Jake, who was standing in his doorway. "It's time to start your morning routine. Why don't you grab your clothes and toothbrush and I'll walk you to the bathroom?"

"I don't want to take a shower, especially in there," Benjamin said. He didn't want to do anything in the unfamiliar shared bathroom.

"Why not?"

"I just don't want to."

"Well, then, how about you get dressed and we'll head down for breakfast?"

Jake closed his bedroom door, and for a moment, Benjamin just sat at the edge of his bed. There were voices outside his door, kids and adults walking past, and in one fierce wave, he missed home. He pulled on his favorite pair of sweatpants and softest, most un-hurting cotton shirt and met Jake in the hallway.

The cafeteria to which Jake walked him was big, with sunlight streaming through a wall of windows. A shorter brick wall reminded Benjamin of the outside of his house, and the room was filled with round tables. Kids—Benjamin quickly counted thirty-one—lined up for their breakfast, grabbing cartons of milk from a silver refrigerator before making their way down the line.

"I want some French toast," Benjamin said.

"Well, today's your lucky day," Jake told him. "I see some French toast right next to the scrambled eggs."

Benjamin leaned over to see, and sure enough, there were fluffy squares of French toast sprinkled with powdered sugar. The tight feeling in his chest relaxed a little but didn't go away completely. He didn't have his train plate. This wasn't his kitchen. Mom and Dad had left him. What was he supposed to do in this place? The more he added up the things that weren't right, weren't normal, about this situation, the less the French toast mattered. How long was he going to be here? Mom and Dad said they would be back in two weeks, but would they really? Maybe they would like life without him more. Without realizing it, he started bouncing on the balls of his feet.

"Benjamin?" Jake's voice was firm and soothing. "Seems

like you might be a little upset. What's going on? Can you tell me what you're feeling right now?"

"DON'T TALK TO ME!" Benjamin screamed. "I DON'T WANT TO BE HERE!"

He no longer noticed the sounds of the room around him—chairs scraping, forks clinking against plates, kids talking, adults talking, doors opening and closing. He felt lost in a gulf of anger and sadness, an overwhelming sense of being left behind, left alone. The boy in front of him in line turned around, and Benjamin screamed, "STOP LOOKING AT ME!" and slapped the boy's tray from his hands, sending it clattering to the ground.

"Okay, Benjamin," Jake said. "I understand you're feeling upset right now. Let's go over here for a bit, and I'll give you some space to calm down."

Benjamin's rage was like a hurricane, swirling through him and out of him, but with no one trying to hold his arms down or yelling back at him or saying, "No trains later if you keep this up," it passed quickly, leaving him feeling exhausted and drained. As usual, he could hardly remember what had set him off; he just had a lingering, unsettling feeling that he'd done something wrong. Suddenly all he wanted to do was sleep.

Ten minutes later, when the room went back to normal, Jake walked Benjamin through getting French toast and milk. "So, Benjamin," he said, "let's talk through what just happened. What do you think was the trigger—the thing that made you upset?"

Benjamin shrugged. "I missed Mom and Dad, but I was mad at them for leaving me here."

"Okay, that's a fair thing to feel. How did you respond to that?"

Benjamin wasn't used to being asked these questions. He didn't think he liked it. "I got mad," Benjamin snapped. "I didn't want to be around people, especially people looking at me."

"What do you think might work better for you when you're upset?" Jake asked. "Some of our kids here ask to take a break sometimes, so they can be alone for a minute and calm down. Do you think that would work for you?"

Benjamin thought about it. He did like to be alone. He nodded. "That might work for me."

Jake smiled. "That's really good to know. Thanks for communicating that to me. Now, why don't we go sit with a couple of other guys in our group?" Jake gestured with a tilt of his chin. "See that table over there? That's Ryan and Joseph."

Ryan was chubby, with dark hair and a white t-shirt, and Joseph was around Benjamin's size with strawberry blond hair and freckles all across his nose and cheeks. Benjamin didn't say anything; he just followed Jake to the table.

"Hey, guys," Jake said, pulling up a chair. "This is Benjamin. He's new to our group here at Genesee Lake School. How about you tell him a little about how our day goes? Maybe run through our regular schedule?"

"We go to school after breakfast," Ryan said. "There are eight of us in the classroom and two teachers. Sometimes we go to the computer lab. I love computers."

Joseph gave Benjamin a quick wave before diving back into his pancakes.

"I'm not hungry," Benjamin told Jake. He pushed his tray away. "And I don't like school."

"Our school is different than the school you're used to,

Benjamin," Jake said. "You might like it more than you think."

Benjamin's homeroom class was smaller than any classroom he'd had in public school. There were only seven other students—four boys and three girls—and three adults. The teacher was tall, with short brown hair and a dark blue shirt, and smiled when she saw him. She said he could call her Ms. Lauren as she led him to a desk.

"This will be your desk, Benjamin," Ms. Lauren said. "If you're not comfortable on the seat or if you'd rather sit on the floor, just let me know. We also have some standing desks for kids who get a little fidgety. Some kids also sit on therapy balls."

Benjamin was surprised. He'd never been in a classroom where kids sat on the floor or stood, but one boy was sitting in front of the rows of desks, and no one made fun of him or told him to get back to his seat. One of the girls had a red cushion on her chair. Another boy was sitting and bouncing on a big blue therapy ball. Someone else was squeezing a squishy ball, like the ones his OT had given him a long time ago. The lights in the class were dim, and there were painted pictures on the wall that Benjamin could tell the students had made.

"Up here is our class schedule, Benjamin," Ms. Lauren said. She pointed to a long laminated block schedule. Each block showed a clock with a different time and then a different subject, like reading and art and science. "This is your homeroom class and your science class. You can see the times you'll be in each subject over here."

Benjamin started to feel overwhelmed with all the new information. He rocked gently back and forth in his chair.

"Okay!" Ms. Lauren said. "Why don't we get started?

Benjamin, we always like to start the day with some deep breathing exercises. It's so important for our bodies that we get good oxygen in our lungs, and breathing deeply helps calm our minds, too."

Benjamin's gaze flicked around the classroom. The other students were fidgeting in their seats, shrugging their shoulders and moving their necks around.

"Let's do volcano breath," Ms. Lauren said. Her voice was low and slow. "We'll start with putting our palms to our hearts and taking a deep breath."

Ms. Lauren closed her eyes and breathed deeply, her chest expanding. The sound of breath filled the room. Uncertainly, Benjamin put his palms to his chest the way everyone else was doing.

"Now let's stretch our arms toward the sky as we exhale," Ms. Lauren said. "Feel how nice that stretch feels. You're warming up your body, getting it ready for the day. Very good."

Benjamin lifted his arms, but he was a little late, because Ms. Lauren was now saying to reach their fingertips toward the walls and bring their palms back to "heart center." Benjamin just sat with his hands in his lap. He didn't like not knowing what to do.

"Great job, everyone," Ms. Lauren said. "Now, how about some guided imagery? Benjamin, I know this is probably all new for you, but for this one, all you have to do is put your head on your desk and close your eyes."

Benjamin looked around. He'd gotten in trouble so many times for doing this in public school. The teachers told him to pay attention, that he was being disrespectful, and their angry voices made Benjamin want to run away. But now all the kids were resting their heads on their arms as if they were going to sleep! Part of him wondered if this was a trick, but he did it anyway.

"Okay, everyone," Ms. Lauren said in her low voice. "We're about to go on a flight over North America. On the count of three, imagine that your chairs are lifting off from the floor. One … two … three! I'm pushing a button, and the roof of this classroom is sliding right off to let us pass. Now we're rising … we're flying above school now, reaching the tops of those tall trees outside. When we look down, we can see cars and grass and people walking."

Benjamin fidgeted in his chair. It was still on the ground. He was having problems imagining he was flying.

"Okay, we're flying higher and higher now. We're high above the United States now. Can you feel the clouds around us? Now, remember our lesson yesterday, clouds are made of drops of water and ice, and there are four main types of clouds: cumulus, cirrus, stratus, and nimbus … "

The guided imagery lasted for about ten minutes, and even though most of Benjamin still felt grounded in this classroom, toward the end he could almost pretend he was flying. It made him feel calmer.

After lunch, when Benjamin and the other students were back in Ms. Lauren's class for Science, something strange happened: Ms. Lauren told the class that she was going to hand out an assessment, and that it was just for her to see where the kids were at, so they shouldn't stress about it. But one boy, who was sitting on a stool, immediately crumpled to the floor. It was as if his body just melted, folding in on itself, and then he was lying in a heap on the ground, screaming and crying. Benjamin blinked. It was like watching himself.

"I DON'T WANT TO TAKE YOUR STUPID ASSESSMENT!" the boy

yelled. He was bigger than Benjamin, and his voice was deeper and loud. He curled in a ball, rocking and pounding the floor with his hands. With one violent roll forward, he hit the ground with his head.

"It's okay, Matt," said the teacher's aide. Immediately, she grabbed a heavy-looking blue blanket from a corner of the room and draped it over his shoulders. He pulled it tightly around himself while the teacher's aide rubbed his back. Meanwhile, Ms. Lauren told the rest of the class to follow her into the "breakout room," a smaller offshoot of the main classroom, to continue their lesson.

"Matt's having a bad day," one girl told Benjamin matter-of-factly. "That happens sometimes. He'll be okay."

By the end of the day, Benjamin was exhausted and over-stimulated, but he had a meeting with Dr. Mike, who was a talking doctor like Dr. James. Melanie, who had come into his class once to see how he was doing, walked Benjamin over to Dr. Mike's office. He sat on a couch, wearing dress pants and a blue button-down shirt like Dad wore, with a striped tie. His eyes were brown and slightly crinkled in the corners, and he told Benjamin to sit anywhere he wanted. Benjamin dropped to the floor and crossed his legs.

"So, Benjamin," Dr. Mike said, "I know we just met, but I'd like to get to know you better. Tell me, how was your first day of school?"

Benjamin shrugged. "School was different than what I'm used to. It was a small classroom with a smaller room to the side. There were only seven other students. We did something called volcano breath, and Ms. Lauren told us to imagine we were flying out of school. That was hard for me. We had science in the afternoon. Science is one of my favorite subjects. A boy got mad, though, and we had to leave the classroom."

"Yeah, that can happen sometimes," said Dr. Mike. "We all get upset, and that's all right. But you know, there are things we can do that help us when we get upset or feel our bodies getting tense. I call them coping tools—we all need them once in a while. Do you ever get upset, Benjamin?"

Benjamin thought for a moment before answering. "Sometimes," he said quietly.

"Well, let's talk a little bit more about that, okay?"

Benjamin intertwined his fingers and pulled them apart as Dr. Mike passed some papers to him. Dr. Mike also had a copy and showed it to Benjamin.

"All right, check this out," Dr. Mike said. "It's real simple and has three parts. The first part has to do with triggers, or things that happen to make you upset, the second part has to do with how your body feels and reacts when you're upset, and the last part is about what you and we can do to help you cope and feel better."

Benjamin looked down. The first page said, "What makes you feel upset?" Beneath the question were a series of pictures. Except for the questions Jake had asked him this morning, Benjamin had never really thought about his moods before—not like this.

"So, Benjamin," Dr. Mike said, "do you see anything on here that makes you upset? Do you get upset when there are too many people around?"

Benjamin nodded. "I hate being with too many people. They can be so loud!"

"Yeah, I can understand that. So do loud noises also bother you?"

"Yes. The bell at my old public school was so loud. I hated that, too."

Dr. Mike asked a few more questions, figuring out that Benjamin also got upset when he was surprised, when his bedroom door was open, and when people yelled or were mean.

"That's very good, Benjamin," Dr. Mike said. "See, we're starting to connect that there are certain triggers that lead to feelings. What do you think about that?"

Benjamin looked down at the papers with their cartoon drawings. He shrugged. "It's different to think about it. I never have before." After a moment, he added, "I like the drawings."

"Yeah, the pictures help a lot of our kids understand things a bit better," Dr. Mike said. "I'm glad they're working that way for you. How about the second page? What happens to your body when you're upset?"

Benjamin roved his eyes over the next page, recognizing a few pictures: cry, hot face, loud voice, swearing, racing heart, breathing hard, running away. It seemed as if he were pointing at all of them, and the more he pointed to, the worse he felt. This must be why he was here. He rocked back and forth on the floor."

"It seems like you might be getting a bit upset," Dr. Mike said. "It's all right, Benjamin. Sometimes it's tough to talk about these things, but it is important."

"I don't want to talk to you," Benjamin said. "I don't want to talk to anyone."

"I know it's hard right now, but how about you look at one last page? This is the really neat part—where we figure out the things that make you feel better. Because remember, it's okay to get upset. The goal is to handle it in a way that doesn't make things rough for others and for us. Okay?"

Benjamin nodded. Maybe he wasn't so different from other people after all; he just hadn't learned these "coping skills." The truth was, though, Benjamin didn't know what made him feel better. Usually he just raged and yelled and hit things until he didn't feel like doing that anymore. These pictures showed things like deep pressure, skin brushing, and special blankets (like the boy in class, Benjamin realized)—and some normal activities, like reading, watching TV, and listening to music. He told Dr. Mike that squeeze balls, finding a quiet place, and taking a walk helped, because he knew he had done those things before, and he remembered feeling better after he did them.

"This is really good. Thanks a ton, Benjamin," Dr. Mike said. "This way, we can help you out when you're feeling upset. We do this for all our kids. What we'll do is put this on a small card for you, and you can carry it in your pocket—kind of like a secret weapon for when you're feeling upset and not sure what to do to feel better. Your staff and teachers will also have a copy of this so they know what to do, too."

Benjamin nodded. "I suppose that sounds okay."

"There are some kids your age playing in the gym," Dr. Mike said, standing. "I was thinking we could go check that out before dinner. These are some of the guys I see weekly for our social problem-solving group. I'm thinking you'd be a good part of the group, too."

"But I hate groups," Benjamin said, thinking of his after-school social skills group.

"Have you had a bad experience in a group in the past?

What was so bad about it?"

"Sean was mean, and I barely ever got a Super Effort sticker or the candy I wanted." Benjamin didn't like thinking about his old group.

"Sounds like it didn't go so well, huh?" Dr. Mike said. "Well, our group is a little different here. We have fun, work on teamwork, and learn to slow down and *think things through*. We also spend some time talking about our coping toolboxes. We'll talk more about that later—but let's go meet the guys and hang out."

Benjamin stared for a moment at Dr. Mike. He was nice. And this did not sound like the other group. Still, Benjamin remembered all the times he had tried to make friends in school—all the laughter and turning away and calling him a nerd or a freak. He'd never 'hung out' with anyone before. He'd probably never have a friend. He wasn't even sure he knew what a friend really was.

"I don't want to," he said, almost angrily. "I don't like these kids. They're weird, and I don't like being here, and I want to call my mom *now*."

"How about we call your mom after we spend some time with the kids?" Dr. Mike asked. "I'd like for you to meet them, even if it's just for a little while."

"No," Benjamin said. "I want to call her *now!*" He hopped off the floor and paced the length of Dr. Mike's office. He felt cagey, wanting to run away.

"All right," Dr. Mike said calmly. "This isn't going to work right now—let's find Melanie and see about that phone call."

Dr. Mike walked to his desk and picked up the phone, reaching Melanie quickly and explaining that Benjamin wanted to make a call. He walked Benjamin over to

Melanie's office, where Melanie was already on the phone with Benjamin's mom.

"He did great in school today," Melanie said brightly, "and he just had a good session with Dr. Mike where they talked about emotional coping strategies. All in all, it was a very positive first day. Now, let me pass you over to Benjamin."

Benjamin snatched the phone from Melanie, still feeling upset, and all he felt when he heard Mom's voice was sadness. Still, talking to her was better than not talking to her, so Benjamin told her about his day and said no when she asked if he liked it there.

"It's all your fault—you and Dad—for putting me here," he said before hanging up and closing himself in his room.

· · ·

The first month Benjamin was at the Genesee Lake School was a difficult one for Marie and Jason. The house was bizarrely quiet without Benjamin's meltdowns, and guiltily—feeling oddly as if he were erasing Benjamin—Jason began spackling and painting the walls his son had damaged most recently. When he was angry, he yanked knick-knacks from the bookshelves and hurled them at the walls, so much so that Jason and Marie had boxed most of those things away. The "Benjamin-proofed" house, as they called it, had a barren, impersonal feel to it.

At first, Marie left the door to Benjamin's room closed, the way he liked it, and turned the light on inside so she could see the strip illuminated beneath the door. A few times, when she couldn't sleep in her bed, she thought of going to sleep outside his door the way she had so many nights before.

"Do you miss him?" Marie asked Jason.

Out of habit, they still talked in the bathroom, though they left the door open and water off these days. Marie sat on the floor with her back against the vanity cabinets.

Jason sighed. "Yes. No. I mean, of course I do—but it's hard to separate him from all the behavior and problems. And I know I don't miss that."

"Are we bad parents?" Marie asked. "Because I feel like a complete failure. Why couldn't we do this right?"

"Look, we've done our best," Jason said, almost fiercely. "That's all any parent can do. But we also have two other kids who need us."

Jason was right. Zach was six and still sleeping with them, and Mandy was loathe to move back from her grandparents' house. Marie knew it would take some time to repair their relationship with Mandy, in particular. Now fourteen, she was at once older than her years and very much a teenager, full of sarcasm that covered up deep hurt. For the first week she was home, the only times Marie or Jason heard her voice was when she was on the phone or talking to her younger brother. She was as loving with Zach as she used to be with Benjamin, before he stole their parents, as she sometimes put it.

"I have an idea," Marie said one afternoon. "Why don't we give your room an overhaul?"

Mandy looked up from the book she was reading. Marie could tell she wanted to keep ignoring her, but curiosity won out. "What do you mean?"

"Well, sometimes it's good to start over," Marie said. "You probably have different taste now than you did when you were twelve. Do you still like the color of your walls?"

They were bright purple, the shade of the geraniums that grew in the front yard.

Slowly, Mandy shook her head. "Are you saying I can re-paint?"

"I'm saying *we* can re-paint. We'll make it a project. What do you say?"

Mandy chewed her bottom lip. After a long pause, she said, "I guess so."

That weekend, Marie and Mandy went to their local hardware store, and Mandy chose two shades for the walls: the top two thirds would be a bright, buttery yellow, and the bottom third would be dove gray. "I'll have to get a new bedspread to match," Mandy said.

Marie laughed. "We'll see."

They spent the afternoon traipsing over the plastic sheeting laid on Mandy's carpet, with Mandy handling the large roller and Marie doing the grunt work of taping and cutting in edges with a brush. Mandy played music from her iPod, none of which Marie knew, and they worked largely without talking. That was okay with Marie. She was overcome with joy, sadness, and guilt at just spending this uninterrupted time with her daughter.

In the evenings, to transition Zach away from sleeping with them, Marie and Jason started reading to him in his own bed. They sat one on each side, letting their youngest child cuddle in or splay out across them as he desired. After reading exactly one book, they told him they loved him and kissed him goodnight.

"When can I come into bed with you again?" he asked.

Jason smiled. "You know the new rule, partner. No earlier than six in the morning."

Six a.m. was a nice compromise. Neither Jason nor Marie minded Zach slipping in beside them for the thirty minutes before their alarms went off. His warm body and steady breathing was as comforting to them, Marie sometimes thought, as they were to him.

Another big change they made was family dinners. When Benjamin was home, the idea of the five of them—or even the four of them, once Mandy was at her grandparents'—sitting down together for a meal was ludicrous. Either Jason or Marie was always occupied with Benjamin while the other fixed Zach a hasty meal, and the adults simply ate what they could when they could. Now, both Jason and Marie felt it was an important addition to their routine—a demonstration of stability and unity.

"Is all this going to change when Benjamin gets home?" Mandy asked one night. Her tone was cynical. "Because if it is, I don't see the point."

"The point is that we spend time together as a family," Jason said. "That's what counts, no matter what happens when Benjamin comes back. And we have to remember that Benjamin is a member of our family, too."

"So it is going to change."

"Of course things will change *some*," Marie said, "but the whole reason your brother is at the Genesee Lake School is so he can learn skills that will make things go better when he comes home. Fewer meltdowns, with a better understanding of his emotions and how to develop relationships."

"Yeah." Mandy rolled her eyes. "I'm sure he'll be rainbows and butterflies."

Marie sighed, looking at Jason. "Maybe not rainbows and butterflies—that's not realistic. But better. Things will be definitely better."

...

"So you're still not wanting to shower, huh?" Melanie asked. "Benjamin, you've been here for two months. The expectation is that kids shower daily, and staff are telling me you have showered about once a week, after a lot of reminders. I'd like to talk that through with you."

Benjamin sat on a chair in the Redwood Activity Room with his arms crossed. He didn't look at Melanie.

"Here's the deal," Melanie said. "Problems pop up in life for all of us. We at GLS follow the 'Think: Kids Collaborative Problem Solving Approach,' because we work together to figure things out—instead of adults just telling you what to do and you maybe doing it. How about we give it a try?"

"It sounds like a trick to get me to do what you want."

"It's not a trick. We want to find a solution that works for you and for us and that is doable. Let's give it a shot and 'think this through.' We'll use this to help." Melanie retrieved a dry erase board from against the wall. "So—it's not going so well at shower time. Benjamin, what's going on?"

"I just don't want to take a shower," Benjamin said. "And you can't make me."

"I'm not saying you have to take a shower, and we are definitely not going to 'make you' take one. I just want to better understand your concern."

Benjamin crossed his arms more tightly. "I don't like this."

"You're doing a great job hanging in there. My job is just to understand your concern about showers. Tell me more about why it has been so hard to shower here."

Benjamin felt a pang as he remembered his bathroom at home. Mandy and Zach used it, too, but it was familiar. After a long pause, he grumbled, "It's like a stranger's bathroom here. I don't know it. It's weird to me, and it's hard to go in there."

Melanie made an *Mmm* noise. "Okay, so what I'm hearing you say is that it's very unfamiliar, not much like the bathroom at home, and that makes it hard to take a shower. Does that sound right?"

"Yeah."

"Okay, great. Thanks for telling me. I feel like I got a good idea of what your concern is about showers."

At the top of the dry erase board, Melanie wrote, "Refusing to shower regularly" with an arrow pointing below to "Shared bathroom is unfamiliar and not like home."

"Okay, so I understand why you're uncomfortable," Melanie said. "The thing is when this shower issue happens, it has an effect on your health and hygiene, which is a big part of our job here. And also ..." Melanie lowered her voice, "I've heard there is a bit of a body odor problem the kids have noticed, and that's been making it harder for them to be near you."

Reflexively, Benjamin turned his nose toward his shoulder and sniffed. "What? You're kidding. Nobody has ever told me that."

"Sometimes it's hard to know what other people are thinking. I wonder if there's something we can figure out so the bathroom feels more familiar to you and more like the bathroom at home, and makes you more comfortable. At the same time, we can make sure your health and hygiene are taken care of and that other kids want to be around you more. Do you have any ideas?"

Benjamin shrugged. "No, I don't, and I really don't care what you guys think."

"Well, we still have a problem to be solved here that is

not going away," Melanie said, "and it's important to take both sides into account for a good solution."

Benjamin couldn't explain why, but he felt like testing this process. "Okay. I have an idea. I say you guys give me twenty bucks every time I take a shower."

Melanie smiled. "Well, every idea is a good idea, Benjamin, but for it to work, it needs to work for you, work for us, and be doable." Melanie referred to the three columns on the dry erase board. "This idea works for you, but it does not work for us, and I know it would not be doable for us to pay you twenty bucks every time you take a shower. Do you have any other ideas?"

This time, Benjamin actually thought about it. What *would* make him less uncomfortable in that bathroom? "What if only I use it?"

Melanie smiled again. "That's an idea, too, and it works for you, but it won't work for us. It's also not doable, because the other kids need to use that bathroom. Nice try, though. Let's keep going and figure something out."

"Well . . ." Benjamin let his breath out in a huff, "what if you guys let me use the same shower and sink all the time? And what if I also get to have my shampoo and soap from home? They smell better."

Melanie beamed. "Well, that's an idea! So what you're saying is that this would work for you because it would make things more familiar and comfortable, and I think this would work for us, because there are never more than three kids in a bathroom at one time, and there are three sinks and showers—so I think they'd be fine with you always using one sink and shower. Plus, I know I could call your mom tomorrow about the shampoo and soap. So it looks like this works for you, works for us, and is doable. Let's give it a shot—what do you think?"

"I want my shampoo really bad."

"Don't worry; we'll take care of it tomorrow."

The next morning, the youth counselors talked to Benjamin before showering, and he chose the sink closest to the window and the middle shower. He stood inside the stall, opening and closing the blue and green plaid shower curtain. At the sink, he turned the faucet on and off, on and off, and splashed some water on his face. He looked at himself briefly in the mirror. His hair was getting long. He moved it over to one side the way Mom used to when he was little. After spending ten minutes in the bathroom, it didn't feel as scary.

The following week, Benjamin was in the gym with Dr. Mike, who had taught him about a 1–5 anxiety scale. Benjamin, Dr. Mike, and Ryan—one of the boys Benjamin had met in the cafeteria on his first day—were playing a game called "Make a Basket, Ask a Question." The gym was airy and bright, with gleaming wood floors, and smelled like citrus and rubber. Benjamin had only been here a few times. He wasn't good at sports and was never picked for any team at his regular school, but Dr. Mike had promised this wasn't a win-or-lose game. It was exactly as it sounded: they took turns shooting the basketball, and whoever made a basket got to ask another person a question. The goal of the game was to "get to know each other better." Dr. Mike said that asking questions was essential to having back and forth conversations, which connected people and helped with relationships, making friends, and making us happier. Benjamin didn't have much practice asking people questions. He usually just told them what he wanted.

Ryan, who also had Asperger's disorder, wasn't good at sports, either. He missed a lot of shots before he made one. One of Dr. Mike's rules was that if you made a shot, the other guys said "Nice shot" and if you missed a shot, the other guys said "Nice try." Dr. Mike made the first shot.

"Nice shot," Ryan said.

Benjamin had already forgotten that rule. "Nice shot," he echoed.

"Thanks, guys," Dr. Mike said. "So, how about this— what's your favorite food?"

Benjamin held the basketball. "French toast with maple syrup."

"Yeah, that does sound pretty good," Dr. Mike said. "How about you, Ryan?"

"I love M&Ms," said Ryan. "Especially the green ones."

"I get that. I'm a chocolate fiend!"

Dr. Mike moved them along to the next shot, and they took turns shooting for a while. Finally, Benjamin made a basket. "Yes!" he cried, as the others told him "nice shot." His shirt was sticking to him. He didn't like that, but he forgot about it as he tried to think of a question. All he could think of were statements: *Steam locomotives are usually classified under the Whyte system. Electric locomotives usually run on steep grades or areas with heavy traffic density.* "Ryan, what's your favorite type of locomotive?" Benjamin finally asked.

Ryan wiped sweat from his forehead. He stared at Benjamin blankly.

Dr. Mike said, "That's a good question. What do you think, Ryan?"

Ryan stood still on the court, chewing his lip for a second. "I don't know. I have no clue."

"Benjamin, Ryan's having a hard time thinking of a

locomotive. Any idea why?" Dr. Mike asked.

Benjamin considered. It was hard to imagine what Ryan thought. "He doesn't like them?"

"That's one possibility," Dr. Mike said. "What's another?"

"Maybe he doesn't have a favorite type of locomotive?"

"Hmm." Dr. Mike nodded thoughtfully. "How could you check that out?"

"I could ask him."

"Great! Go ahead and do that."

Benjamin looked at Ryan, formulating his question. "Do you have a favorite locomotive?"

Ryan shook his head. "No, I don't. Trains are okay, but I really don't know much about them. But I love cars!"

Benjamin looked at Dr. Mike, who was watching them with a smile. "Great job figuring out what Ryan was thinking by asking him a question."

When Benjamin next asked Ryan what his favorite *car* was, Ryan said, "The 1926 Bentley Speed Six Tourer. It was the most successful racing Bentley."

They played for another thirty minutes, during which they asked one another's favorite colors, favorite engines, and favorite movies. It was fun.

At the end of the game, Dr. Mike said, "You guys did a great job today. What did you learn about each other? Let's try to think of three things each."

Benjamin said he'd learned that Ryan liked cottage cheese, his dad was an attorney, and he was from Illinois, and Ryan said he'd learned Benjamin had a sister and a brother, wanted a new telescope for Christmas, and was from Minnesota.

Ryan said matter-of-factly, "I think maybe Benjamin and I could be friends."

Benjamin was surprised. He could have a friend? What did that mean? He rocked a little on his feet because he was caught off guard, but for once, it was in a good way.

At six-thirty on the dot the following night, Benjamin made his way to the activity room. Melanie had told him there was a steam locomotive documentary on TV tonight, and all day Benjamin had been thinking about it. The rest of the guys were okay with it being on, too. The TV was off when Benjamin entered the room, even though two other boys were sitting in there. One was clicking Legos into place, while the other sat in a chair against the wall, engrossed in a book about Japanese etiquette.

Benjamin clicked channels until he found History. It was just starting—he'd made it in time! The screen filled with an image of a black locomotive rolling down the track, thick plumes of steam rising above it. A male British voice, carefully modulated, began talking about the golden age of steam, and Benjamin sat down on the floor in front of the TV. The kid clicking Legos stopped what he was doing and came over to watch it with Benjamin. They watched, riveted, for the next twenty minutes—until suddenly the channel changed! History went to *Law and Order*, which went to *How It's Made*, where it remained while Benjamin whirled around, stunned. A boy named Austin, a little older than Benjamin, held the remote control tightly.

"You've been watching your train crap forever," he said. "Give someone else a turn."

"Austin, the show is over in ten minutes," one of the youth counselors said. "You can watch what you want after."

Austin raised the volume on *How It's Made*. "It's my turn. Benjamin can get over it."

"No!" Benjamin said. "It's free time. I get to see *The Golden Age of Steam!*" The familiar heat swelled in Benjamin's chest, and he jumped to his feet. "CHANGE IT BACK!" he shouted. "CHANGE IT BACK!"

Just then, Melanie came into the room. She looked between the two boys and then at the others, who were still engaged in their activities but looking a little concerned. "Hey, guys, what's going on here?"

"He's hogging the TV, and it's my turn!" Austin said.

"Did you ask Benjamin if he would share the TV?" Melanie asked.

"No."

Benjamin threw himself on the ground, rocking back and forth and slapping the carpet hard with his palms.

"Benjamin, you seem very upset right now," Melanie said. "Remember what we've talked about before? Those coping tools?"

He heard Melanie's voice from a great distance away, and he didn't care about it right then, but he *remembered* caring about it, so he struggled to call his mind to the current moment. Reaching into his pocket, Benjamin felt the laminated card with his anxiety scale and coping tools. A four meant, "It's pretty hard for me right now. My body feels wiry and tense, brain is getting fuzzy, and I need to take a break or take a walk with someone safe."

With intense effort, eyes clenched shut, Benjamin said, "Go for a walk. I want to go for a walk with you now." He forced himself to his feet and walked quickly and stiffly past Austin, who was standing behind Melanie, and out of the room. Melanie walked quietly beside him down the hallway and out the main doors outside. She was doing something called "walk and don't talk." They had talked about this strategy before when he was calm.

The sun was lowering over the tall trees—such a deep green, with gold tips—and the air was turning cool and felt good against his flushed cheeks. He walked along the sidewalks, at first still angry—*furious*—and wanting to hit Austin and watch his trains, but slowly, slowly he started to forget about the documentary and come back to where he was, right now.

"Benjamin," Melanie said quietly, "remember the three big stress busters?"

With effort, Benjamin nodded. "Relaxation, distraction, and, I don't know … the other one."

"Exercise is the other one. Why don't we try some breathing exercises for relaxation as we walk?"

In a low, slow voice, Melanie guided him to breathe in through his nose and out through his mouth, measured breaths in and out.

"Let's count our breaths," Melanie said. She breathed in through her nose and after she exhaled said, "Count with me now. *One …*"

Benjamin breathed and counted with her. He had been panting, but now he thought of his big breath through the nose, oxygen going all the way into his body, and released through the mouth, back to the trees and plants and grass, and finally he stopped walking and turned to Melanie.

"How are you feeling now?" Melanie asked softly.

"I feel better," he said. "Thank you. I don't like getting upset. I know people think I do, but I really don't. It just happens, and I throw a fit sometimes."

"Remember, it's okay to get upset—anger isn't the enemy. It's all about the intensity and how we handle it." Melanie pulled out the safety tool card. "Okay, so on a scale of one to five, where were you in the group room?"

"A four."

"And where are you now?"

Benjamin stopped to listen to his body. He wasn't a one yet, but the walking and breathing had helped. "A two," he said, which meant his body felt a little jittery and his brain jumpy, and that taking some deep breaths would help.

"Great job showing self-control and calming yourself down," Melanie said, smiling. "That was a tough situation, and you worked through it by focusing on your thinking and feelings."

Benjamin nodded. Then he did something he didn't do very often: he smiled. He hadn't reached a five. He *always* reached a five. Sure, Melanie had helped him, but he had done most of the work, and it had ended well. He had problem-solved. He had coped. And he was proud.

. . .

When Marie and Jason sat with Melanie and Dr. Mike in the Genesee Lake School's conference room, it was with familiar emotions—fear, worry—as well as some new ones: Relief. Pride. Hope. They'd come to visit Benjamin every two weeks like clockwork, and while it took a while to see noticeable improvement, they'd been able to go from on-grounds visits to off-grounds visits. They'd even spent the night in a nearby hotel once with only one small meltdown that lasted about thirty seconds. Benjamin was, for the first time in a *very* long time, manageable.

"As we've discussed on the phone," Melanie said, "Benjamin has made great strides over the last six months.

Perhaps the biggest is . . ." She looked at Dr. Mike. "He's saying he has made a friend."

"A friend?" Jason repeated.

"Well, it's a positive peer relationship and not a friend-ship rooted on a deep emotional connection," Dr. Mike explained. "But it's based on mutual respect and recognition that there is somebody else who thinks like him and has a lot of the same interests. Benjamin and Ryan spend a lot of time together talking about engines and mechanical things. They like to draw pictures for each other as well. For all kids, this is huge. He feels a connection to someone besides his family, and from what we've heard, this has not happened before?"

"*Never*," Marie said. "I mean, he tried, sometimes, to make friends, but it never worked."

Jason shook his head. "It's just so far from where we came . . ."

Marie was crying before she realized it. "It's almost more than I dared to hope. Is that terrible?"

"Not at all," Dr. Mike said. "When Benjamin first came, it was your reality. Friendships might always be a struggle, but we know that connections and relationships are important for all people in life. Finding people with common interests will be a way for Benjamin to develop more relationships over time."

"I thought kids could only learn these kinds of things when they're very young," Jason said. "Benjamin is twelve now."

"Well, intervening during the early years in life is extremely important," Dr. Mike replied, "but like Dr. Stanley Greenspan said, 'It's never too late to develop foundations in relating, communicating, and thinking.' We believe that here. No matter someone's age, positive change can still happen."

"He's made some other good strides here as well," Melanie added with a smile.

"Like what?" Marie asked.

"Well, as we told you on the phone, we were having a difficult time getting him to take daily showers. We tackled that pretty well through some collaborative problem solving—we got his concern, told him ours, and then found a solution that worked for everyone involved. Pretty simple, too—he uses the same sink and shower, and we have the same shampoo and soap here as he does at home."

"You really didn't have to threaten him or take something away to have him take a shower?" Jason asked.

"No." Melanie shook her head. "Those approaches tend not to solve the problem for good, because they don't address the concerns. Negative consequences have their place but can sometimes contribute to explosive behavior and fracture the relationship. We try to get kids to practice thinking and problem-solving skills here instead."

Marie thought back to the days of Benjamin's special education and after-school social skills group. "We were always told to use consequences and sticker charts and things like that. They worked for a while, but all he cared about was what he could earn."

"And melted down if he didn't," Jason added wryly.

"We always try to keep in mind that each of our kids is going to be thirty someday," Dr. Mike said, "so we need to figure out what skills he lacks and teach them so he can be a better problem solver when he is older. Sticker charts might generate some external motivation, but they don't get the job done long term if the kid doesn't have the skills. Benjamin, as you know, has significant difficulty with emotion regulation, planning, social skills, and inflexible or rigid thinking. A sticker chart wouldn't address any of those things."

"So the showering," Marie said. "That's taken care of?"

Melanie smiled. "When these kids make connections and friends, and realize that we want to work *with* them and not *against* them, we see them become more open to trying new things. They're more accepting of new situations and more responsive to our adult concerns—which are linked to health, learning, safety, and how the child's behavior affects others. Benjamin has been keeping up with his hygiene routine and showering regularly. Maybe not every day—he still says it seems weird and different, so we're trying some things—but with some reassurance and reminders, it happens every other day on average. That's a great improvement."

"What about his meltdowns?" Marie asked.

"Let me take a look." Melanie opened a folder and ran a finger down the page. "The last meltdown, with screaming and hitting the floor, was ... two weeks ago."

"*Two weeks?*" Marie and Jason exclaimed.

"Two weeks."

"That's ... incredible," Marie said. A part of her felt a pang of old guilt, wishing she'd been able to achieve these results for her child on her own, but she recognized now that there was no shame in asking for help when it was so desperately needed.

We work with the kids and staff on understanding their cycle of rumbling, rage, and recovery, based on the work of Brenda Smith-Myles," Dr. Mike said. "As we've talked about, those are the three stages of meltdowns. Benjamin's triggers are the same as they've always been, but we try to be mindful that the best place to intervene is during rumbling; at rage, most kids are not very rational. For Benjamin, the rumbling is when he looks down, rocks back and forth, paces, maybe claps his hands—and that's when we remind him of his coping strategies and incorporate sensory strategies as well. We've seen it make a significant difference in reducing the frequency of rage episodes."

Marie and Jason nodded, taking it all in.

"We have to remember that kids with significant emotion regulation problems—like your son, who is receiving psychotropic medication for a diagnosed mood disorder—don't *like* being upset or showing explosive behavior," Dr. Mike said. "And they're certainly not doing it on purpose."

"I know he doesn't like getting so upset all the time," Marie said. "He just looks miserable!"

"It must be miserable," Melanie agreed. "The key when he goes home is for you to remember that consistent challenging behavior, including explosive behavior, is the product of underdeveloped skills in flexibility, frustration tolerance, and problem-solving, plus the task or demand we are 'throwing at' them."

"So, for example," Dr. Mike added, "you would expect a kid who has difficulty shifting from one mindset or task to another to struggle when we require him to ... what?"

"Well ..." Marie said, looking at Jason, "when you require him to shift mindset. Like if he has a lot of transitions during the day."

"Exactly."

"So these are things we can incorporate when he comes home?" Jason asked.

"These are the things you *should* incorporate at home," Dr. Mike said. "We believe they can be of significant help to Benjamin and the whole family."

"You're not on your own, though," Melanie said. "How about we talk prior to his next home visit about some of the basics to try?"

Marie felt a swell of relief and gratitude. "Thank you. What about the future here, then?"

"Well, now that Benjamin has made some nice progress in our center building, we think it's time to look at a transition to a less restrictive environment," Melanie said. "A GLS group home. The one we have in mind is right at the end of the school's driveway, so it's still close, but Benjamin will have much more independence. He'll have a roommate and daily chores, learn how to do his own laundry, help prepare meals, and be responsible for getting himself ready each morning."

"He'll learn many of the basic living skills that will help him successfully transition back to your home," Dr. Mike said. "How do you two feel about that?"

"Will he be safe? That's my number one concern," Marie said. It hadn't been that long ago, after all, that Benjamin was punching through walls, climbing out windows, being hospitalized. What if he wasn't as ready for this as they thought? What if he raged and decided to just … take off?

"We have at least two staff with the kids all the time," Melanie said. "That's the same coverage as here at the center building. More importantly, if we didn't feel that Benjamin was *already* safe—not liable to injure others or himself—we wouldn't even think about transitioning him. Transition to the group home occurs slowly, as well, and at his pace—so we'll start with short visits, spending time with the other kids, maybe go see a movie with them, give him some pictures of the group home so it's more familiar, things like that."

Marie looked at Jason, and he nodded. "That sounds good," Marie said. "Let's give it a try."

. . .

At the group home, everyone had chores. They washed dishes, dusted the appliances, swept and mopped the floors, and cleaned the bathrooms. And they all did their own laundry.

Monday afternoon was Benjamin's turn for laundry. It was his first time washing his own clothes. At home, Mom always picked up the hamper from his bathroom, and the next time Benjamin saw his clothes, they were folded up again in his drawers. At the Genesee Lake School dorms, he just threw his laundry down a chute.

One of the group home staff, Dan, showed Benjamin everything before. There were instructions taped up in the laundry room, twelve steps with pictures, the way Benjamin liked to see things. He began, as shown, with sorting his clothes: whites with white, darks with darks, colors with colors. Benjamin smiled, sitting on the laundry room floor surrounded by like-colored piles of clothes. This was actually a little fun. He decided to start with whites and build up to the darker colors, so he measured the detergent—spilling just a little, he'd wipe that up—and poured it and the whites in the washer. He closed the lid, squinted at the instructions, and set it to wash. For a moment, he stood listening to the rumble of the machine. He knew he was supposed to leave the wash, but he felt protective of it. Scooting his piles of clothes to one side of the small area, he sat leaning up against them. Benjamin wanted to stay in the room from beginning to end, and Dan came in every so often to make sure he was doing all right.

After laundry, it was dinnertime, and Benjamin's chore was to wash dishes. He hated washing dishes—the crusty food and sticky sauces disgusted him, but Dan gave him a pair of gloves that made the situation better.

It was all pretty overwhelming at first. Benjamin didn't quite know what to do with the new independence, but he eventually grew comfortable with his routine. He woke up to his own alarm. He dressed, ate breakfast, and walked to school with staff if it was a nice day in the mornings. Sometimes, if he ran late, he was anxious when he got to homeroom, so he grabbed a fidget toy or a squishy ball and used those until he felt better. (He also had those in his room at the group home.) Ms. Lauren's guided imagery helped. When he closed his eyes and imagined flying over North America, there were times he could really see the shadows of clouds on land, and it slowed his breathing right down.

For science class one day, Ms. Lauren brought in water from Genesee Lake. She prepared slides that the students would look at under a microscope. There was an air of excitement to the morning as they waited for Ms. Lauren and Miss Jean—the teacher's aide—to arrange the slides under the different microscopes.

"I've never used a microscope before!" said a girl named Emily.

"Can I see a show of hands?" Ms. Lauren asked. "Who here has used a microscope?"

Only one hand out of eight went up, and it was not

Benjamin's. He liked science—there were right and wrong answers, facts. Benjamin's brain understood facts. But he had never gotten to use a microscope in public school. Now he was fidgety and hyper and went to the corner of the classroom to grab a fidget toy while he waited. Slipping his fingers in and around the rubbery ovals stilled his nerves so that he wouldn't rock back and forth too much on his therapy ball.

"Okay, everyone," Ms. Lauren said. "Let's each choose a microscope, and I'll explain how to use them."

The three adults guided the students to different microscopes, and Benjamin peered down at the slide. It was maybe one inch wide by two inches long, tinged greenish from the water. He felt slightly disappointed. There was nothing special about his slide.

Ms. Lauren explained how to put their eyes near but not touching the lenses and how to adjust the scope with little dials on the sides. She told them that lake water had a variety of organisms living in it and that the microscopes would help them see what was invisible to the naked eye.

"Like a superpower!" Matt rang out.

Benjamin cracked a smile as other students laughed. He was fidgety again. He wanted to see what was on his slide!

At first, everything just looked a cloudy green, and Benjamin felt a stronger rumbling of dissatisfaction. Then Miss Jean came over and helped him work the microscope, and all of a sudden, right there before Benjamin's eyes was something he had never seen before—a creature with a tubular body and waving tentacles like an octopus! He gasped and pulled away from the microscope.

"I have something!" he cried. "I have something! I have something!"

Ms. Lauren crossed the room, and other students gathered around him. "Hang on, guys, let's give Benjamin some space," Ms. Lauren said. "We can all take a turn." She smiled at Benjamin and leaned over to take a look in his microscope. "Well, look at that! That's called a hydra."

Benjamin was immediately fascinated. He wanted to know everything about the hydra. Maybe there was information in their science books, or he could borrow a book from the library or go to the computer lab.

"I want to see!" Emily said.

She pressed to the front of the group, and Benjamin intercepted her. "It's my microscope. Go back to yours."

Emily stared at Benjamin for a moment before her green eyes welled with tears.

Benjamin stared back at her. He had talked with Dr. Mike about "scoping it out"—using his eyes, ears, and brain to pay attention to clues in himself and others to solve problems. Someone having tears usually meant they were upset. Benjamin had done something that made Emily upset. He puzzled for a minute. "It's my microscope," he said again, less certainly.

Ms. Lauren asked, "Benjamin, why don't you want Emily to look in your microscope?"

"I want to look at the hydra some more."

"What would be a way both of you, and even the rest of the class, can take a look?

"I don't know."

"Remember, when we have a problem in life, the options are usually *ask for help*, *meet halfway*, or *do it a different way*. Which one might work here?"

Benjamin rocked back on his heels. "I guess we could take turns."

"Okay, so doing it a different way is the best option." Ms. Lauren smiled. "Great. How about we let Emily and whoever else wants to take a peek, and when they're done, you'll be able to look at it for the rest of the class."

Benjamin stared at his blue sneakers that Mom and Dad had sent from home. He felt like crying, but instead he went to his desk and picked up the fidget toy again. He played with that until everybody had taken a turn looking at his hydra.

"Thanks," Emily said, smiling at him.

Benjamin was pleased and smiled back. When Ms. Lauren said the microscope was his again, he ran to it and didn't stop staring until it was time for his next class. Waiting hadn't been so bad after all. Not great, but not horrible as he would have predicted.

After school, Benjamin went to the computer lab. He was shown to a station, where he immediately went online and typed "hydra" into Google. He clicked on the images, first the ones that looked like his slide, and then the ones that were like diagrams, with arrows pointing at different body parts: hypostome, penduncle, basal disk. Words Benjamin had never heard before. He was riveted.

"Benjamin," he heard. "Hey—Benjamin."

He made himself turn around. Ryan was sitting at another computer station. He waved.

"I saw a hydra today," Benjamin said. "Hydra are organisms belonging to the phylum cnidaria. They do not have exoskeletons. They have six tentacles and a mouth called a hypostome."

"Tentacles are cool!" Ryan said before turning back to his own computer.

Benjamin called his parents after chores the way he did every night. Most of the time they answered, but sometimes they didn't. Benjamin didn't like it when the phone rang out. It made him upset and sad and fearful, so he still cried. But he tried hard not to yell at other people or hit things. The laminated card in his pocket helped Benjamin fight those urges.

Tonight, Mom told him she had big news: he would be going home in one month.

"Home?" Benjamin repeated. "But I'm home now."

Mom was quiet on the line. In an odd voice, she said, "You'll be coming home with us, I mean. Don't worry. We'll make sure everything and everyone is ready for you."

• • •

The district had agreed to fund fifteen months of treatment for Benjamin at the Genesee Lake School and the group home, and that time went by much faster than Marie and Jason had expected. All of a sudden, it was a Saturday in early spring, and they were pulling up to the white clapboard house Benjamin called home.

"Here we go, Marie. Are you ready?" Jason asked. "Are *we* ready?

Marie looked at her husband, whom she finally felt she knew again, and felt a flash of fear. As much as Benjamin needed a routine, the rest of the family did, too. And they'd finally established one, with equal time and attention spent on the two kids living at home. She recalled Mandy's question: "Is all this going to change when Benjamin gets home?" The truth was that Marie didn't know how much would change. She wanted to shrivel up at the thought of their home life returning to what it had been before GLS—chaotic and uncertain. All she and Jason could do was work hard with the GLS in-home team helping with transition, be diligent about helping Benjamin maintain the tools and techniques he'd learned, and change their own behavior to match. That meant no trying to talk, reason, discipline, or threaten him with punishment during his rages. They knew now that he needed space and, most importantly, for them to remain calm and supportive. The best thing they could do was remind him of his stress or anxiety scale and his coping strategies throughout the day, and make sure they were also posted in the house. The whole family should know about them, be consistent, and follow the routine as well as they could. They would also not try to eliminate train books or videos; instead, they would allow access to Benjamin's special interest—not twenty-four/seven, but they recognized now that trains served a purpose for him. They were a source of pleasure, a way to overcome anxiety, and a way for Benjamin to demonstrate intelligence.

The other major thing they had to remember was that *behavior is a form of communication*. No matter how inexplicable or arbitrary Benjamin's actions seemed, he was trying to tell them something, and it was an opportunity for exploration and understanding for everyone. For example, so many of his meltdowns occurred when he felt chaotic and unbalanced. Benjamin needed structure, routine, and certainty, so his daily and weekly schedules would be posted in the house and in his bedroom, and everyone in the family would help him follow them. Marie and Jason would refrain from hounding him to do chores, instead focusing on the expectation and the reasons for them, and then use collaborative problem solving to "think it through" when problems came up. The in-home team would also teach them how to use strategies such as understanding the importance of antecedent/behavior/consequence patterns, specific praise, social narratives, comic strip conversations, and of course, visual supports in the home.

As the long list ran through Marie's head, she forced a smile for Jason. "Ready? I don't know about that. But willing? Of course. Thank goodness for the in-home assistance we'll have."

Benjamin's funding also included five hours a week of in-home support, as well as respite for two weekends a month at GLS. In the month since Marie had told Benjamin he was coming home, they had worked with Karen—a woman far more knowledgeable and experienced than her twenty-eight years would imply—to learn some of the strategies used at the Genesee Lake School. Karen had also already spoken to Benjamin's new teachers at the public school, helping them understand Asperger's disorder and Benjamin's specific behaviors and support strategies. She had explained the plan that was followed at the Genesee Lake School and would be followed in the home. While a part of Marie was terrified because of her memories of school, she was also hopeful. Maybe, just maybe, this would be the start of a new normalcy for their family . . . even if it wasn't other families' normalcy.

"Let's get our son," Marie said.

The group home was quietly busy with kids going about their daily activities. Melanie and Dan, the group home manager, were waiting with Benjamin, who stiffly pulled a rolling suitcase from his bedroom. He looked around the living room, as if committing it to memory.

"They had a farewell party for me last night," Benjamin said to Marie and Jason. He still didn't like to make a lot of eye contact, but a small smile tweaked his lips.

"A party!" Marie said. "That's wonderful. Did you have fun?"

Benjamin nodded. "Ryan came, even though he lives in a different group home. We're going to write letters to each other."

Marie fought tears as Melanie caught her eye, smiling. "That's a great idea, Benjamin," Melanie said.

For a moment, they all stood there silently. Then Jason stepped toward Benjamin and hugged him. Benjamin was stiff, but he patted Jason's back in return.

"Everyone is looking forward to seeing you," Jason said, pulling away.

Benjamin nodded. He looked quickly at Melanie and Dan. "Thank you," he said. "I'm ready to go home now."

When their goodbyes were said, Jason loaded Benjamin's suitcase in the car, and the three of them climbed inside. Marie found herself surprisingly nervous on the drive. She chatted constantly, feeling as if she were courting her own son, trying to convince him that he would like it at home. Of course, Benjamin had stayed with them about six times over the last three months, and Mandy and Zach had gone to visit him several times as well. Marie and Jason both felt it was important that he feel connected to their home as a family, but Marie didn't know how successful their efforts had actually been.

"Mandy and Zach are so excited to see you," Marie said. "They stayed with Grandma and Grandpa while we came up to get you, but they'll be back in time for dinner tomorrow."

"We've talked a lot with Melanie about things," Jason added. "We've written your daily and weekly schedule out for you and put it on your door and in the living room, just like at GLS. That way, you'll always understand what's going to happen and what to expect."

"And if things don't always go the way I expect," Benjamin said, "it's not always a big deal."

Marie and Jason exchanged surprised glances. "Well, that's right," Marie said, smiling. She glanced back at Benjamin, and he met her eyes quickly before looking back out the window.

"Six o'clock is the time we eat at the group home," he said. "I don't like washing dishes, but I use gloves. Those guys can really make a mess."

"We'll figure out a family chore routine between the five of us," Marie said.

That night, the three of them sat on the living room couch watching the History Channel. Benjamin was between them, focused and engaged, his eyes bright. Marie had sensory tools available, and Benjamin ran his fingers lightly over a fidget toy. Though history was something Benjamin had always enjoyed, and thus his behavior now was not necessarily indicative of the norm, Marie let herself relax a little. Her son was home, almost thirteen years old, and seemed happy. Maybe not super smiley happy the way a typically developing child might be coming home from camp, but there was an element of contentment to him that he had certainly been missing before.

The next day, Mandy and Zach arrived home after school (which Benjamin would start the following week) with trepidation. Marie and Mandy had grown closer in the months Benjamin had been away, and she had tearfully confessed her fear that Benjamin would be "chosen" over her again. "I don't want to be mad at him," Mandy said. "I love him, and I know it's not his fault. But I just wish you guys had noticed my honor roll over Benjamin's tantrums for once."

Zach's memories, meanwhile, were vague but strong. He seemed to associate fear with Benjamin without a vivid sense of what caused it. Once, he had asked Jason, "Is Benjamin going to hurt me?" and Jason wrapped his arms around him and promised they would not let that happen.

Benjamin was now taller than Mandy, and he stiffly accepted the quick hug she gave him.

"I'm glad you're home," she said.

"Me, too," Zach added.

"Thank you. It's nice to be here."

At six, Marie called everybody into the kitchen for dinner. Mandy helped Marie serve the food, Zach set out the plates, and Benjamin filled glasses with water. Marie felt both overwhelmingly tense, as if poised for crisis, and overwhelmingly joyful as her family of five—all five, together!—ate dinner. Mandy talked about her driver's education class, Zach brought up an upcoming field trip to the aquarium, and to everyone's surprise, Benjamin talked about an organism he had seen under a microscope in science class.

"It lives in water," he said, looking at his plate. "Like fish."

It took a moment to sink in: Benjamin was responding to Zach. He was trying to relate his hydra to Zach's aquarium trip. Marie's eyes welled up. Whatever the future held, she was sure it would be brighter than the years they'd left behind.

. . .

When Benjamin was twenty-one years old, he got his high school diploma. His parents took him to choose a frame, and he picked a smooth black one with a little gilded gold. They hung it in the living room, and he often stared at it with pride. School had not been easy, but he had done it.

He also had a job! Three days a week, he worked at the public library, putting books back on shelves. He was part of a work program through the Department of Vocational Rehabilitation. His head librarian called him "focused and responsible," and Benjamin had actually developed a new library inventory management system that kept more accurate, efficient track of books than before. It gave Benjamin pleasure to help organize the library. Organizing was simple, black and white, and Benjamin's mind intuitively understood it. He recognized now that this was a skill he had that other people did not. This, too, made him proud. Having Asperger's disorder meant that he had strengths, too, just like everyone else; it didn't always have to make life more difficult for him.

Twice a week, Benjamin took martial arts classes in Tae Kwon Do. He had started a year ago at the suggestion of his GLS in-home staff, and he looked forward to the days he put on his dobok and went to the center. Benjamin liked the order and structure of the classes, and he felt more self-confident than he had before. He could protect himself if he needed to, but the most important part for him was the five tenets of Tae Kwon Do: courtesy, integrity, perseverance, self-control, and indomitable spirit. They were good guides for his life—especially the tenet of self-control. In Tae Kwon Do, it was defined as the ability to exert one's will over inhibitions, impulses, and emotions. Benjamin liked that.

His in-home staff still came over for one-hour weekly sessions to support him, but Benjamin was told that would be ending now that he was twenty-one. On days he felt overwhelmed or anxious—usually when he had been thrown a curveball—he walked to the train tracks by his house. The moment he neared them, he felt the same rush of happiness and calm he had as a kid, running there from school. He sat in the shade of great white pines and waited for the Burlington Northern Santa Fe or CSX trains to roll by, and he practiced volcano breath as they roared hotly past him. One after another, they went ... origin to destination, origin to destination.

HOW THESE BOOKS WERE CREATED

The ORP Library of disabilities books is the result of heart-felt collaboration between numerous people: the staff of ORP, including the CEO, executive director, psychologists, clinical coordinators, teachers, and more; the families of children with disabilities served by ORP, including some of the children themselves; and the Round Table Companies (RTC) storytelling team. To create these books, RTC conducted dozens of intensive, intimate interviews over a period of months and performed independent research in order to truthfully and accurately depict the lives of these families. We are grateful to all those who donated their time in support of this message, generously sharing their experience, wisdom, and—most importantly—their stories so that the books will ring true. While each story is fictional and not based on any one family or child, we could not have envisioned the world through their eyes without the access we were so lovingly given. It is our hope that in reading this uniquely personal book, you felt the spirit of everyone who contributed to its creation.

ACKNOWLEDGMENTS

The authors would like to thank the following team members at Genesee Lake School and ORP who generously lent their expertise to this book: special education teacher Sheri Dunham; residential services director Sarah Goralski; admissions director Stephanie Koster-Peterson; and clinical coordinator supervisor Melissa Stoffel. Your time, perspective, passion, humor, and wisdom helped us bring this story to life—and help children like Benjamin every day.

We would also like to extend our heartfelt gratitude to the families who shared their journeys with us. The courage, ferocity, and love with which these parents shepherd their children through their lives is nothing short of heroic. Mark, Liz, Andy, and Kevin Blutstein; Susan Gallacci and Alex Spurgeon; Lois Menis, CJ Menis, and family; and the Taylors: Jeremy and Christian, and Hunter, Jacob, Jona, and Josh—thank you for inviting us into your stories. Your families are our inspiration.

And to readers of this book—the parents committed to helping their children, the educators who teach those children skills needed for independence, the therapists who shine a light on what can be a frighteningly mysterious road, and the schools and counties that make the difficult financial decisions that benefit these children—thank you. Your work is miraculous.

JEFFREY D. KRUKAR, PH.D.

BIOGRAPHY

Jeffrey D. Krukar, Ph.D. is a licensed psychologist and certified school psychologist with more than 20 years of experience working with children and families in a variety of settings, including community based group homes, vocational rehabilitation services, residential treatment, juvenile corrections, public schools, and private practice. He earned his Ph.D. in educational psychology, with a school psychology specialization and psychology minor, from the University of Wisconsin-Milwaukee. Dr. Krukar is a registrant of the National Register of Health Service Providers in Psychology, and is also a member of the American Psychological Association.

As the psychologist at Genesee Lake School in Oconomowoc, WI, Dr. Krukar believes it truly takes a village to raise a child—to strengthen developmental foundations in relating, communicating, and thinking—so they can successfully return to their families and communities. Dr. Krukar hopes the ORP Library of disabilities books will bring to light the stories of children and families to a world that is generally not aware of their challenges and successes, as well as offer a sense of hope to those currently on this journey. His deepest hope is that some of the concepts in these books resonate with parents and professionals working with kids with disabilities, and offer possibilities that will help kids achieve their maximum potential and life enjoyment.

KATIE GUTIERREZ

BIOGRAPHY

Katie Gutierrez believes that a well-told story can transcend what a reader "knows" to be real about the world—and thus change the world for that reader. In every form, story is transformative, and Katie is proud to spend her days immersed in it as executive editor for Round Table Companies, Inc.

Since 2007, Katie has edited approximately 50 books and co-written five—including two of the ORP Library of disabilities books. She has been humbled by the stories she has heard and hopes these books will help guide families on their often-lonely journeys, connecting them with resources and support. She also hopes they will give the general population a glimpse into the Herculean jobs taken on so fiercely by parents, doctors, therapists, educators, and others who live with, work with, and love children such as Benjamin.

Katie holds a BA in English and philosophy from Southwestern University and an MFA in fiction from Texas State University. She has contributed to or been profiled in publications including *Forbes*, *Entrepreneur* magazine, *People* magazine, *Hispanic Executive Quarterly*, and *Narrative* magazine. She can't believe she's lucky enough to do what she loves every day.

JAMES G. BALESTRIERI

BIOGRAPHY

James G. Balestrieri is currently the CEO of Oconomowoc Residential Programs, Inc. (ORP). He has worked in the human services field for 40 years, holding positions that run the gamut to include assistant maintenance, assistant cook, direct care worker, teacher's aide, summer camp counselor, bookkeeper, business administrator, marketing director, CFO, and CEO. Jim graduated from Marquette University with a B.S. in Business Administration (1977) and a Master's in Business Administration with an emphasis in Marketing (1988). He is also a Certified Public Accountant (Wisconsin—1982). Jim has a passion for creatively addressing the needs of those with impairments by managing the inherent stress among funding, programming, and profitability. He believes that those with a disability enjoy rights and protections that were created by the hard-fought efforts of those who came before them; that the Civil Rights movement is not just for minority groups; and that people with disabilities have a right to find their place in the world and to achieve their maximum potential as individuals. For more information, see *www.orp.com.*

ABOUT ORP

Oconomowoc Residential Programs, Inc. is an employee-owned family of companies whose mission is to make a difference in the lives of people with disabilities. Our dedicated staff of 2,000 employee owners provides quality services and professional care to more than 1,700 children, adolescents, and adults with special needs. ORP provides a continuum of care, including residential therapeutic education, community-based residential services, support services, respite care, treatment programs, and day services. The individuals in our care include people with developmental disabilities, physical disabilities, and intellectual disabilities. **Our guiding principle is passion:** a passion for the people we serve and for the work we do. For a comprehensive look at our programs and people, please visit *www.orp.com*.

ORP offers two residential therapeutic education programs and one alternative day school among its array of services. These programs offer developmentally appropriate education and treatment for children, adolescents and young adults in settings specially attuned to their needs. We provide special programs for students with specific academic and social issues relative to a wide range of disabilities, including autistic disorder, Asperger's disorder, mental retardation, anxiety disorders, depression, bipolar disorder, reactive attachment disorder, attention deficit disorder, Prader-Willi Syndrome, and other disabilities.

Genesee Lake School is a nationally recognized provider of comprehensive residential treatment, educational, and vocational services for children, adolescents, and young adults with emotional, mental health, neurological, or developmental disabilities. GLS has specific expertise in Autism Spectrum Disorders, anxiety and mood disorders, and behavioral disorders. We provide an individualized, person-centered, integrated team approach, which emphasizes positive behavioral support, therapeutic relationships, and developmentally appropriate practices. Our goal is to assist each individual to acquire skills to live, learn, and succeed in a community-based, less restrictive environment. GLS is particularly known for its high quality educational services for residential and day school students.

Genesee Lake School / Admissions Director
36100 Genesee Lake Road
Oconomowoc, WI 53066
262-569-5510
http://www.geneseelakeschool.com

T.C. Harris School is located in an attractive setting in Lafayette, Indiana. T.C. Harris teaches skills to last a lifetime, through a full therapeutic program as well as day school and other services.

T.C. Harris School / Admissions Director
3700 Rome Drive
Lafayette, IN 47905
765-448-4220
http://tcharrisschool.com

The Richardson School is a day school in West Allis, Wisconsin that provides an effective, positive alternative education environment serving children from Milwaukee and the surrounding communities.

The Richardson School / Director
6753 West Roger Street
West Allis, WI 53219
414-540-8500
http://www.richardsonschool.com

RESOURCES

Attwood, Tony. *Asperger's Syndrome: A Guide for Parents and Professionals*. London, England: Jessica Kingsley Publishers, 1998.

Attwood, Tony. *The Complete Guide to Asperger's Syndrome*. London, England: Jessica Kingsley Publishers, 2007.

Buron, Kari D. & Curtis, Mitzi. *The Incredible 5-point Scale: Assisting Students with Autism Spectrum Disorders in Understanding Social interactions and Controlling Their Emotional Responses*. Shawnee Mission, KS: Autism Asperger Publishing Co., 2003.

Clark, Rick. "Cognitive Experiential Group Therapy" (Workshop presented at ODTC, Oconomowoc, Wisconsin, December 19, 2011).

Gray, Carol. *Comic Strip Conversations*. Arlington, TX: Future Horizons, 1994.

Greene, Ross W. *The Explosive Child*. New York: Harper Collins Publishers, 2005.

Greene, Ross W., and Ablon, J. Stuart. *Treating Explosive Kids: The Collaborative Problem-Solving Approach*. New York: The Guilford Press, 2006.

Greenspan, Stanley, and Wieder, Serena. *Engaging Autism: Using the Floortime Approach to Help Children Relate, Communicate, and Think*. Cambridge, MA: Da Capo Press, 2006.

Smith Myles, Brenda, and Southwick, Jack. *Asperger Syndrome and Difficult Moments: Practical Solutions for Tantrums, Rage, and Meltdowns*. Shawnee Mission, KS: AAPC, 2005.

"Autism Internet Modules," *http://www.autisminternetmodules.org*

"Interdisciplinary Council on Developmental and Learning Disorders," *http://www.icdl.com*

"IDEA – Building the Legacy: IDEA 2004," *http://idea.ed.gov*

"Massachusetts Department of Mental Health-Restraint/Seclusion Reduction Initiative: Safety Tool," *http://www.mass.gov/dmh/rsri*

"Think:Kids, Rethinking Challenging Kids," *http://www.thinkkids.org*

ASPERGER'S DISORDER

Meltdown and its companion comic book, *Melting Down*, are both based on the fictional story of Benjamin, a boy diagnosed with Asperger's disorder and additional challenging behavior. From the time Benjamin is a toddler, he and his parents know he is different: he doesn't play with his sister, refuses to make eye contact, and doesn't communicate well with others. And his tantrums are not like normal tantrums; they're meltdowns that will eventually make regular schooling—and day-to-day life—impossible. Both the prose book, intended for parents, educators, and mental health professionals, and the comic for the kids themselves demonstrate that the journey toward hope isn't simple ... but with the right tools and teammates, it's possible.

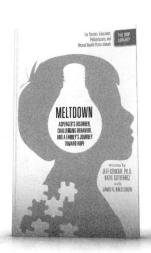

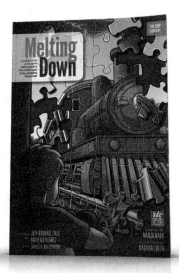

MELTDOWN

ASPERGER'S DISORDER,
CHALLENGING BEHAVIOR,
AND A FAMILY'S JOURNEY
TOWARD HOPE

MELTING DOWN

A COMIC FOR KIDS WITH
ASPERGER'S DISORDER AND
CHALLENGING BEHAVIOR

AUTISM SPECTRUM DISORDER

Mr. Incredible shares the fictional story of Adam, a boy diagnosed with autistic disorder. On Adam's first birthday, his mother recognizes that something is different about him: he recoils from the touch of his family, preferring to accept physical contact only in the cool water of the family's pool. As Adam grows older, he avoids eye contact, is largely nonverbal, and has very specific ways of getting through the day; when those habits are disrupted, intense meltdowns and self-harmful behavior follow. From seeking a diagnosis to advocating for special education services, from keeping Adam safe to discovering his strengths, his family becomes his biggest champion. The journey to realizing Adam's potential isn't easy, but with hope, love, and the right tools and teammates, they find that Adam truly is *Mr. Incredible*. The companion comic in this series, inspired by social stories, offers an innovative, dynamic way to guide children—and parents, educators, and caregivers—through some of the daily struggles experienced by those with autism.

MR. INCREDIBLE

A STORY ABOUT AUTISM,
OVERCOMING CHALLENGING
BEHAVIOR, AND A FAMILY'S FIGHT
FOR SPECIAL EDUCATION RIGHTS

INCREDIBLE ADAM
AND A DAY WITH AUTISM

AN ILLUSTRATED STORY
INSPIRED BY SOCIAL NARRATIVES

BULLYING

Nearly one third of all school children face physical, verbal, cyber, and social bullying on a regular basis. For years, educators and parents have searched for ways to end bullying, but as that behavior becomes more sophisticated, it's harder to recognize and to stop. In *Classroom Heroes* and its companion comic book, Jason is a quiet, socially awkward seventh grade boy who has long suffered bullying in silence. While Jason's parents notice him becoming angrier and more withdrawn, they don't realize the scope of the problem until one bully takes it too far—and one teacher acts on her determination to stop it. Both *Classroom Heroes* and its companion comic recognize that in order to stop bullying, we must change our mindset. We must enlist not only parents and educators but the children themselves to create a community that simply does not tolerate bullying. Jason's story demonstrates both the heartbreaking effects of bullying and the simple yet profound strategies to end it, one student at a time.

CLASSROOM HEROES

ONE CHILD'S STRUGGLE WITH BULLYING AND A TEACHER'S MISSION TO CHANGE SCHOOL CULTURE

CLASSROOM HEROES

COMPANION CHILDREN'S BOOK

FAMILY SUPPORT

Schuyler Walker was just four years old when he was diagnosed with autism, bipolar disorder, and ADHD. In 2004, childhood mental illness was rarely talked about or understood. With knowledge and resources scarce, Schuyler's mom, Christine, navigated a lonely maze to determine what treatments, medications, and therapies could benefit her son. In the ten years since his diagnosis, Christine has often wished she had a "how to" guide that would provide the real mom-to-mom information she needed to survive the day and, in the end, help her family navigate the maze with knowledge, humor, grace, and love. Christine may not have had a manual at the beginning of her journey, but she hopes this book will serve as yours.

CHASING HOPE
YOUR COMPASS FOR A NEW NORMAL

NAVIGATING THE WORLD
OF THE SPECIAL NEEDS CHILD

REACTIVE ATTACHMENT DISORDER

An Unlikely Trust: Alina's Story of Adoption, Complex Trauma, Healing, and Hope, and its companion children's book, *Alina's Story,* share the journey of Alina, a young girl adopted from Russia. After living in an orphanage during her early life, Alina is unequipped to cope with the complexities of the outside world. She has a deep mistrust of others and finds it difficult to talk about her feelings. When she is frightened, overwhelmed, or confused, she lashes out in rages that scare her family. Alina's parents know she needs help and work endlessly to find it for her, eventually discovering a special school that will teach Alina new skills. Slowly, Alina gets better at expressing her feelings and solving problems. For the first time in her life, she realizes she is truly safe and loved . . . and capable of loving in return.

AN UNLIKELY TRUST
ALINA'S STORY OF ADOPTION, COMPLEX TRAUMA, HEALING, AND HOPE

ALINA'S STORY
LEARNING HOW TO TRUST, HEAL, AND HOPE

Also look for books on Prader-Willi Syndrome and children and psychotropic medications coming soon!